King Solomon's Ring

King Solomon's Ring

New Light on Animal Ways

Rafeal Mechlore

Leader Enterprises

CONTENTS

INDEX

INTRODUCTION

In the domain of human information, the investigation of the creature world has consistently involved a critical and enthralling space. The secrets of creature conduct, correspondence, and insight have captivated thinkers, naturalists, and researchers for quite a long time. These investigations have improved how we might interpret the complicated woven artwork of life on The planet, offering bits of knowledge into the astounding variety of animals that share our planet. One name that stands apart unmistakably throughout the entire existence of understanding creature ways is that of Konrad Lorenz, a visionary researcher and ethologist whose work has revealed new insight into the cryptic universe of creatures and their methodologies.

The title of this book, "Ruler Solomon's Ring: New Light on Creature Ways," bears a secretive reference to a relic from scriptural legend. Rumors have spread far and wide suggesting that Lord Solomon had an enchanted ring with the engraving "Everything good or bad must come to an end," which enriched him with the insight to figure out the dialects of birds and creatures. While the ring of Ruler Solomon could stay a question of legend and old stories, the ring of Konrad Lorenz — figurative however significantly genuine — held the way to opening the mysteries of creature conduct.

In these pages, we leave on an excursion to investigate the life and work of Konrad Lorenz, a man whose spearheading bits of knowledge and revelations significantly affect the investigation of ethology — the logical discipline committed to figuring out creature conduct. Lorenz's work rose above the domain of the scholarly community and saturated mainstream society, affecting our impression of the collective of animals and uncovering the complexities of the normal world in manners that were already unimaginable.

The account of Konrad Lorenz is one of logical interest, fastidious perception, and an enduring energy for understanding the unpredictable examples that oversee the way of behaving of animals going from subterranean insects to gorillas. A story traverses both the scholarly scene of twentieth century science and the profoundly human undertaking to fathom the world we share with our kindred earthlings.

This book is a recognition for the getting through tradition of Konrad Lorenz, a man whose work has made a permanent imprint on the areas of science, brain research, and zoology, and whose impact keeps on resonating in the investigation of creature conduct today.

It likewise fills in as an encouragement to dive into the dazzling universe of creature conduct, where we look to uncover the secrets of correspondence, territoriality, mating, parental consideration, and the complexities of overall vibes in the collective of animals. In our excursion, we won't just investigate the vital bits of knowledge and disclosures of Lorenz yet in addition think about their more extensive ramifications for how we might interpret the regular world and our place inside it.

Konrad Lorenz: The Man Behind the Ring

To see the value in the meaning of Konrad Lorenz's work, understanding the man behind the logical achievements is fundamental. Konrad Lorenz was brought into the world on November 7, 1903, in Vienna, Austria. He was a naturalist, ethologist, ornithologist, and productive creator. Lorenz's initial life was set apart by a profound association with nature, an interest with untamed life, and a curious brain that would later shape his noteworthy examination.

Growing up, Lorenz had a close connection with creatures. He noticed their ways of behaving, noticed their characteristics, and fostered a significant love for the creature world. He was especially attracted to waterfowl, an interest that would prompt a portion of his most huge revelations in the area of ethology. His advantage in creatures was sustained by his family, particularly his dad, Heinrich Lorenz, a noticeable doctor, and his mom, who shared his affection for nature.

Lorenz's scholastic process was no less amazing. He sought after a doctorate in medication at the College of Vienna, where he was profoundly impacted by crafted by Sigmund Freud and Charles Darwin. His initial vocation followed a to some degree wandering way, including his experience as a painter and a concise period as a clinical specialist. It was during this period that he came to see the value in the convergence of workmanship and science, an appreciation that would later appear in his definite, imaginative delineations of creatures and their ways of behaving.

During the 1930s, Lorenz's life took a critical turn when he started concentrating on the way of behaving of birds, especially greylag geese. His careful perceptions and imaginative examinations drove him to plan the idea of engraving, a peculiarity where youthful creatures bond with and gain from the main moving item they see, commonly their parent. Engraving would become perhaps of Lorenz's most persuasive thought, and his earth shattering work on this theme acquired him global acknowledgment.

Lorenz's experiences were not restricted to the lab. He was an adroit onlooker of the normal world, leading hands on work that uncovered the complexities of creature correspondence, the elements of social orders, and the components of mate choice.

His exploration stretched out to different species, including fish, birds, and warm blooded creatures, giving a complete comprehension of the manners in which creatures connect with their current circumstance and with each other.

All through his life, Lorenz remained profoundly associated with the creature world. He really focused on a large group of animals at his home, tenderly known as "Ethology Station." It was here that he directed a considerable lot of his trials and developed a climate where creatures and people could collaborate in a common space, offering one of a kind bits of knowledge into interspecies connections.

Konrad Lorenz's work was not without its contentions and moral inquiries. His relationship with the Nazi system during The Second Great War and his stressed relationship with other unmistakable ethologists of his time added complex layers to his inheritance. In any case, his logical commitments and the effect of his work on how we might interpret creature conduct can't be put into words.

The Meaning of Ethology

The expression "ethology" begins from the Greek word "ethos," signifying "character" or "custom." Ethology is the logical investigation of creature conduct, enveloping a great many ways of behaving from taking care of and mating to correspondence and social communications. While the perception of creatures has been a piece of human life for centuries, the formalization of ethology as a logical discipline is somewhat later, and a lot of its improvement can be credited to the spearheading work of Konrad Lorenz.

Ethology is unmistakable from different areas of science and brain research in its attention on the way of behaving of creatures in their regular environments. Not at all like research center based examinations, which frequently look to comprehend conduct in controlled conditions, ethologists mean to grasp how creatures act in their normal environmental elements. This approach is established in the acknowledgment that creatures' ways of behaving have developed after some time as versatile reactions to their particular surroundings and environmental specialties.

One of the principal principles of ethology is the possibility that way of behaving, similar to some other organic attribute, is dependent upon regular determination. From the perspective of ethology, creature ways of behaving are not simply irregular activities; they are results of developmental cycles, molded by the need to make due and imitate. Ethologists look to figure out a definitive and general reasons for these ways of behaving. Extreme causes allude to the developmental purposes behind the way of behaving, while general causes include the prompt triggers or systems that produce the way of behaving.

Ethology has extended how we might interpret creature conduct in significant ways. It has uncovered the variety of methodologies that creatures utilize to explore the difficulties of life, from searching for food and tying down mates to raising posterity and framing social designs. By valuing these ways of behaving, we gain experiences into the perplexing trap of cooperations that characterize the normal world.

The Intricacy of Creature Conduct

The set of all animals is an exceptionally assorted and complex embroidered artwork of life. It envelops animals that fly through the sky, swim in the profundities of the sea, creep on the woods floor, and wander the huge savannas. While the sheer assortment of species is faltering, what is maybe much more amazing is the rich mosaic of ways of behaving showed by these organic entities.

Consider, for example, the many-sided moves of bumble bees, which convey the area of nectar-rich blossoms to their hive mates. Or on the other hand the intricate melodies of humpback whales that cross a large number of miles to raise and conceive an offspring. Contemplate the trained collaboration of subterranean insects, indefatigably rummaging for food and safeguarding their provinces against gatecrashers. Consider the enthusiastic romance ceremonies of birds of heaven, where guys perform elaborate showcases to draw in females. These are only a couple of instances of the endless ways of behaving that have developed in the collective of animals.

The variety and intricacy of creature conduct bring up major issues: For what reason do creatures act the manner in which they do? How would they speak with one another? What drives their regional questions and social pecking orders? How would they pick their mates, and what procedures do they utilize to guarantee the endurance of their posterity? These inquiries structure the center of ethology and have been vital to crafted by researchers like Konrad Lorenz.

In the pages that follow, we will travel through the different features of creature conduct, every section devoted to a specific subject. We will investigate the perplexing manners by which creatures impart, guarantee and shield domains, take part in romance and mating customs, raise their young, and structure social bonds. From the perspective of Lorenz's work, we will acquire a more profound comprehension of the components and capabilities behind these ways of behaving, and we will reveal the more extensive ramifications of this information for our comprehension own might interpret human way of behaving, society, and our relationship with the normal world.

The Significance of Creature Conduct

Concentrating on creature conduct isn't just a scholarly pursuit; it has significant ramifications for how we might interpret the world and our place inside it. The experiences earned from ethology offer us a new point of view on the complex associations between every living animal, rising above the limits of species. Understanding creature ways empowers us to see the value in the marvels of the regular world, cultivates a feeling of obligation toward our kindred occupants of the planet, and illuminates our own way of behaving and choices as people.

The investigation of creature conduct, most importantly, permits us to see the excellence and intricacy of life on The planet. It uncovers the complicated examples, the shocking transformations, and the striking variety of living creatures. By understanding the ways of behaving of creatures, we gain a more profound appreciation for the rich embroidery of life, rousing a feeling of marvel and wonderment that has enraptured naturalists and wayfarers since the beginning of time.

Besides, the investigation of creature conduct has significant ramifications for protection and environmental mindfulness. As we come to comprehend the jobs that different species play in their environments and the difficulties they face in an impacting world, we are better prepared to secure and save the regular living spaces of these animals. Ethology is a fundamental instrument for saving biodiversity and guaranteeing the drawn out wellbeing of our planet.

In our own lives, the experiences from ethology offer significant examples. From the perplexing moves of bumble bees, we get familiar with the force of viable correspondence and collaboration. From the regional questions of lions, we gain bits of knowledge into the elements of authority and ordered progression. The commitment of parental consideration in different species shows us penance and the obligations of raising the future. By concentrating on the creature world, we find matches with our own way of behaving, manufacturing a more profound association with the regular world and a more significant appreciation for our place inside it.

Exploring the Excursion Ahead

As we set out on this investigation of creature conduct, it is essential to recall that while we may not have a mysterious ring that awards us the capacity to comprehend the dialects of birds and creatures, we have something similarly strong — the capacity to notice, learn, and value the marvels of the regular world from the perspective of science and sympathy.

Every section in this book will dig into an alternate feature of creature conduct, offering a mix of logical bits of knowledge, enthralling stories, and provocative reflections. From the romance customs of birds to the systems of parental consideration in the collective of animals, we will travel through the many components of creature conduct, directed by the insight of Konrad Lorenz and the voices of the animals who share our planet.

Our objective isn't just to commend crafted by a visionary researcher yet additionally to ignite a more profound interest in our general surroundings. The investigation of creature conduct is a continuous excursion, with new revelations constantly growing our comprehension. An excursion welcomes us to clarify some pressing issues, notice the world with an open-minded perspective, and value the miracles of the collective of animals.

We welcome you to go along with us on this excursion, to dig into the profundities of Lord Solomon's Ring, to look for new light on creature ways, and to interface with the astounding variety of life that encompasses us eventually. In doing as such, we honor the tradition of Konrad Lorenz as well as embrace the getting through secret and magnificence of the normal world that he so vigorously esteemed and looked to comprehend.

1. **The Enigmatic King Solomon's Ring**

The account of Lord Solomon's Ring is one that has caught the creative mind of individuals for a really long time. It is a story of insight, enchantment, and an association with the normal world that rises above human getting it. While the actual ring stays a legend, the folklore and imagery encompassing it offer an intriguing look into the human craving to understand and control the perplexing behaviors that most people find acceptable.

The Legend of Lord Solomon's Ring

Lord Solomon is a noticeable figure in the scriptural and verifiable stories of a few societies. He is known for his unbelievable insight, abundance, and the development of the Main Sanctuary in Jerusalem. In any case, his relationship with a mystical ring has most captivated narrators and researchers from the beginning of time.

As indicated by legend, Lord Solomon was presented with a radiant ring that bore an extraordinary engraving: "Everything good or bad must come to an end." This apparently basic expression held the way in to a significant comprehension of the world and its fleetingness. The ring, supposedly, permitted Lord Solomon to speak with creatures, giving him the capacity to figure out their dialects and the mysteries of the normal world.

The thought of an opposite lord with the animals of the Earth is a subject that reverberates across different societies and strict practices. The legend of Lord Solomon's Ring isn't bound to scriptural texts but on the other hand is viewed as in Islamic, Jewish, and Ethiopian legend. In these records, the ring is portrayed as an image of shrewdness, modesty, and the momentary idea of human life.

In the Islamic practice, for example, Solomon's ring isn't simply a device for talking with creatures yet in addition a strong relic used to control jinn, extraordinary creatures in Islamic folklore. This multi-layered understanding of the ring represents its importance in different social settings.

The Imagery of the Ring

The ring's engraving, "Everything good or bad must come to an end," is an impression of a crucial reality of life: temporariness. It typifies that everything is transient, and no state, whether upbeat or troubled, endures until the end of time. This idea, established in old insight, is a widespread topic that has showed up in different structures on the planet's strict and philosophical customs.

The ring represents the grasping that influence, riches, and natural belongings are transient and, eventually, don't characterize an individual's worth. It addresses the fleetingness of human existence and the certainty of progress, an idea that has been investigated in the lessons of different otherworldly practices, including Buddhism and Emotionlessness.

The capacity to comprehend and speak with creatures in the story is additionally profoundly emblematic. It recommends a profound association among human-kind and the regular world, a subject that has been investigated in many societies and legends. In old legends and animistic convictions, people were frequently portrayed as having a profound association with the animals of the world collectively. The ring, in this way, turns into a scaffold between the human domain and the universe of creatures, implying the reliance of every single living being.

Ethology and the Journey for Figuring out Creature Ways

While Lord Solomon's Ring stays a legend, the craving to comprehend and speak with the creature world is a lot of a genuine and persevering through pursuit. Ethology, the logical investigation of creature conduct, means to unwind the secrets of the set of all animals, offering experiences into how different species impart, mate, raise their young, and interface with their surroundings.

One of the vital figures in the area of ethology is Konrad Lorenz, whose work established the groundwork for our cutting edge comprehension of creature conduct. Lorenz's spearheading research centered around engraving, a peculiarity where youthful creatures bond with and gain from the main moving item they see, frequently their parent. Lorenz's work with birds, especially greylag geese, uncovered the mind boggling examples and ways of behaving inside the creature world and offered logical clarifications for peculiarities that were once the stuff of fables and legend.

As it were, Lorenz's work and the investigation of ethology should be visible as a cutting edge investigation of the topics encapsulated by Lord Solomon's Ring. While we might not have a mystical ring that permits us to straight-forwardly speak with creatures, the logical investigation of creature conduct awards us a method for grasping the intricate language of the animals of the world collectively. It permits us to acquire bits of knowledge into the ways of behaving, correspondence, and social designs of the animals with whom we share our planet.

The Conundrum of Creature Conduct

The universe of creature conduct is a domain of unending marvel and intricacy. Creatures show many ways of behaving that have advanced over centuries as versatile reactions to their particular surroundings. These ways of behaving serve different capabilities, including searching for food, getting mates, a safeguarding area, and raising posterity.

The variety of creature ways of behaving is astounding. Think about the complicated mating ceremonies of birds, where guys participate in intricate presentations to draw in females. Or on the other hand the specialized techniques for bumble bees, who dance to pass the area of nectar-rich blossoms on to their hive mates. Consider the regional questions of lions, where the endurance of a pride is in question. These ways of behaving are not arbitrary; they are results of transformative cycles that have formed them over the long haul.

For instance, engraving, an idea established in Lorenz's work, makes sense of how youthful creatures bond with and gain from their parental figures. On account of greylag geese, Lorenz's well known explore involved a gathering of goslings that engraved on him, following him as though he were their parent. This basic yet significant way of behaving is a transformation that guarantees the youthful geese get the essential consideration and insurance during their weak beginning phases of life.

Ethology and Its Bits of knowledge

Ethology gives a structure to grasping a definitive and general reasons for creature conduct. Extreme causes are the developmental explanations behind a way of behaving, making sense of why it exists in any case. General causes allude to the prompt triggers or components that produce the way of behaving. The investigation of ethology looks to disentangle both a definitive and general causes, revealing insight into the significant associations between creature ways of behaving and the conditions where they developed.

One of the most striking parts of creature conduct is the broadness of species it incorporates. Ethologists concentrate on a great many animals, from bugs to warm blooded creatures, and from birds to fish. This variety offers experiences into the differed techniques that creatures utilize to get by and duplicate.

The investigation of ethology additionally uncovers the fundamental standards and shared characteristics in creature conduct. For instance, the idea of territoriality is pervasive in the animals of the world collectively, with numerous species showing ways of behaving to guarantee, guard, or offer domain. Understanding the reasons and components behind regional way of behaving permits us to see the value in the methodologies creatures utilize to tie down their admittance to assets and to shield their posterity.

Moreover, the investigation of mate determination gives significant experiences into the complex and frequently elaborate romance customs of different species. Ethologists research the elements impacting mate decision, from actual qualities to social showcases, and the compromises creatures make in choosing their accomplices.

Parental consideration is one more entrancing part of ethology. The commitment and methodologies utilized by guardians to raise their young can be seen in different species, going from vertebrates like elephants and lions to birds like penguins and hawks. By concentrating on parental consideration, we gain a more profound comprehension of the penances and obligations that accompany supporting the future.

The Proceeding with Mission for Understanding

The area of ethology, similar to any logical discipline, is an excursion of revelation. While much has been realized, there is still an incredible arrangement that stays obscure. The regular world is a huge and complex embroidery, and the investigation of creature conduct is a continuous journey for understanding.

Lately, ethology has developed and incorporated with different disciplines, growing comprehension we might interpret the complexities of creature conduct. Scientists have saddled cutting edge innovation to notice and examine ways of behaving in their regular environments. Hereditary investigations have extended our understanding of the hereditary underpinnings of conduct, and neuroscience has revealed insight into the neurological cycles that drive creature activities.

Besides, the investigation of creature conduct isn't bound to the scholarly community; it has critical genuine applications. It illuminates preservation endeavors by assisting us with grasping the ways of behaving of jeopardized species and the effects of natural surroundings annihilation. It likewise has down to earth suggestions in creature farming, animal government assistance, and, surprisingly, in upgrading our associations with buddy animals.

The Tradition of Ruler Solomon's Ring

The legend of Ruler Solomon's Ring, with its engraving "Everything good or bad must come to an end," perseveres as a sign of the fleetingness of life and the reliance of every living being. It urges us to perceive the worth of intelligence, modesty, and our association with the regular world.

Konrad Lorenz, a researcher of striking knowledge and enthusiasm, might not have had an otherworldly ring, yet he opened the secrets of creature conduct through cautious perception and thorough examination. His heritage lives on in the area of ethology, motivating us to proceed with the mission for understanding the creature ways that advance our reality.

As we venture through the pages of this book, investigating the complexities of creature conduct, we are reminded that the confounding Ruler Solomon's Ring might be a legend, however the getting through quest for information about the regular world is a lot of a reality. Our mission to comprehend creature conduct and its suggestions for how we might interpret the world and ourselves is a demonstration of the getting through interest of mankind, a journey that welcomes us to appreciate and safeguard the secrets and miracles of the regular world.

2. ## The Pioneering Work of Konrad Lorenz

Konrad Lorenz, a name inseparable from the area of ethology, remains as one of the most powerful researchers of the twentieth 100 years. His spearheading work in understanding creature conduct has not just reshaped our view of the normal world yet has likewise offered significant experiences into the mind boggling manners by which creatures impart, adjust, and flourish in their surroundings.

This investigation digs into the life, commitments, and getting through tradition of Konrad Lorenz, a man whose significant interest and fastidious perceptions perpetually changed the investigation of creature conduct.

Early Life and Impacts

Konrad Lorenz was brought into the world on November 7, 1903, in Vienna, Austria, into a family with a profound appreciation for nature and the outside. His dad, Heinrich Lorenz, was an unmistakable doctor, and his mom shared his enthusiasm for the normal world. Experiencing childhood in this climate, Lorenz fostered an early interest with natural life, particularly birds.

Lorenz's initial impacts were mixed, going from crafted by Charles Darwin and Sigmund Freud to writing, theory, and workmanship. He showed a distinct fascination with the convergence of science and style, a trademark that would later appear in his definite and creative outlines of creatures and their ways of behaving.

Advancement of Lorenz's Hypotheses

Lorenz's logical excursion started with a physician certification from the College of Vienna, however his tendency towards creatures won't ever wind down. He set out on examinations in zoology and was significantly impacted by crafted by Oskar Heinroth, a trailblazer in the area of ethology. Ethology, the logical investigation of creature conduct, would turn into the foundation of Lorenz's profession and his enduring inheritance.

Lorenz's initial examinations centered around the life structures and physiology of creatures, which permitted him to foster a strong groundwork in natural science. Notwithstanding, it was his interest with the mind boggling conduct of creatures, especially birds, that would drive him into the universe of ethology. His perceptions of creatures in their regular habitats set before him a way of disclosure that would perpetually impact the manner in which we comprehend and value the collective of animals.

Ethology and Its Effect

Ethology addresses a takeoff from conventional research facility based examinations, as it looks to grasp the way of behaving of creatures in their normal living spaces. Lorenz was a critical figure in laying out this methodology, stressing the significance of noticing creatures in their local surroundings to acquire a genuine comprehension of their ways of behaving. This qualification permitted ethologists to see the value in that ways of behaving have advanced after some time as versatile reactions to explicit natural specialties.

Lorenz's work in ethology was instrumental in moving mainstream researchers' viewpoint on creature conduct. He contended that the way of behaving of creatures was not irregular however was well established in the developmental tensions looked by species over centuries. Lorenz recommended that by concentrating on these ways of behaving, we could open the secrets of variation and endurance in the animals of the world collectively.

Key Commitments and Exploration Strategies

Lorenz's work is portrayed by its fastidious perception and inventive trial plans. He is maybe most popular for his notable examination on engraving, an idea he originally portrayed during the 1930s. Engraving is a peculiarity where youthful creatures bond with and gain from the main moving item they see, ordinarily their parent.

In quite possibly of his most well known explore, Lorenz worked with greylag geese. He saw that goslings engraved on the primary moving article they saw, which was many times Lorenz himself. The engraving system prompted goslings following Lorenz as though he were their mom, showing the significant impact of early encounters on creature conduct.

This work on engraving uncovered that the bond framed among parent and posterity was not just a consequence of maternal consideration but rather was profoundly imbued in the science and conduct of the creatures. Lorenz's bits of knowledge into engraving gave an establishment to understanding how creatures learn and adjust to their surroundings and how these ways of behaving have developed as methodologies for endurance.

Ethological Experiences into Intrinsic Way of behaving

One of the critical commitments of Konrad Lorenz to ethology was his investigation of intrinsic way of behaving. Inborn ways of behaving are those that creatures are brought into the world with and don't have to learn through experience. Lorenz contended that a few ways of behaving are designed into a creature's science because of regular choice.

He proposed the idea of fixed activity designs, which are inborn ways of behaving set off by unambiguous boosts. These ways of behaving are profoundly generalized and happen in a grouping that is normal for the species. An illustration of a proper activity design is the egg-recovery conduct of the graylag goose. At the point when a mother goose sees an egg outside her home, she naturally moves it back into her home, regardless of whether it isn't her own egg. Lorenz's work on fixed activity designs featured the job of hereditary qualities in shaping creature conduct.

The Investigation of Creature Correspondence

One more critical region of Lorenz's exploration was the investigation of creature correspondence. He was especially intrigued by the vocalizations and non-verbal communication that creatures use to pass data on to each other. Lorenz's perceptions of creature correspondence were noteworthy, as they uncovered the perplexing manners by which creatures trade data and keep up with social designs.

One of his renowned investigations included jackdaws, a kind of crow. Lorenz found that jackdaws had explicit calls to declare the disclosure of food, and different jackdaws would answer by running to the area. This correspondence system was crucial for their endurance, as it empowered them to coordinate in scrounging and safeguarding their domain.

Lorenz's exploration on creature correspondence shed light on the mind boggling manners by which creatures pass on data about food sources, likely dangers, and social orders. These discoveries highlighted the significance of successful correspondence in the animals of the world collectively and its part in significantly shaping way of behaving and social designs.

The Meaning of Lorenz's Work

Konrad Lorenz's work significantly affected how we might interpret creature conduct and its job in the regular world. His examination uncovered that creature conduct isn't erratic yet is a consequence of development and variation. This point of view tested the predominant thought that creature conduct was simply scholarly and could be molded completely by natural elements.

Lorenz's bits of knowledge into engraving, inborn way of behaving, and correspondence gave a structure to understanding the complicated ways of behaving showed by creatures in their regular territories. His careful perceptions and creative trials uncovered the secret complexities of the set of all animals, exhibiting that ways of behaving were well established in science and had developed to meet the particular necessities of every species.

Moreover, Lorenz's work overcame any barrier between the logical investigation of creature conduct and the more extensive public's enthusiasm for the regular world. His connecting with composing and capacity to pass the miracles of the set of all animals on to an overall crowd made him an unmistakable science communicator. Lorenz's well known works and talks added to a developing consciousness of the excellence and intricacy of the creature world.

Ethology's Impact on Current Science

The effect of Konrad Lorenz's work reaches out a long ways past his lifetime. Ethology, as a logical discipline, has proceeded to develop and prosper, molding how we might interpret the animals of the world collectively and its interconnectedness with the human world.

Present day ethologists expand upon Lorenz's central thoughts, integrating cutting edge innovations, for example, video recording, hereditary examination, and neuroscience to dive significantly more profound into the secrets of creature conduct. This multidisciplinary approach has empowered specialists to disentangle the brain components that underlie conduct, examine the hereditary premise of specific ways of behaving, and investigate the effects of ecological changes on creature populaces.

Ethology has likewise assumed a critical part in preservation endeavors, as specialists apply how they might interpret creature conduct to safeguard jeopardized species and save biodiversity. By fathoming the ways of behaving of creatures in their regular habitats, researchers can distinguish the particular dangers that these animals face and foster procedures to moderate them.

The Moral and Philosophical Ramifications

Lorenz's work and the area of ethology have brought up significant moral and philosophical issues in regards to our relationship with the collective of animals. The acknowledgment of natural ways of behaving and the organic underpinnings of creature conduct has prompted a more profound enthusiasm for the inherent worth of every species.

Lorenz's work difficulties customary human-centric perspectives that accentuate human transcendence. It features the intricacy and lavishness of the creature world, as well as the interconnectedness of every single living being. Ethology has prodded conversations on creature government assistance, morals, and our obligations as stewards of the regular world.

3. **The Quest for Understanding Animal Behavior**

The investigation of creature conduct has been a wellspring of interest, interest, and marvel for people from the beginning of time. Our mission to grasp the complexities of how animals, incredible and little, explore their surroundings, convey, and collaborate with each other has powered logical request, tested our assumptions, and extended our enthusiasm for the normal world. This investigation digs into the rich embroidered artwork of creature conduct, the trailblazers who have progressed our comprehension, and the getting through mission to understand the personalities of non-human creatures.

The Interest with Creature Conduct

From the earliest long periods of human civilization, individuals have wondered about the ways of behaving of the creatures with whom they share the planet. Our predecessors noticed the relocations of birds, the regional questions of vertebrates, and the complexities of bug social orders. These perceptions frequently tracked down articulation in old stories, folklore, and strict convictions, as creatures were enriched with emblematic and mysterious importance.

In antiquated societies, the ways of behaving of creatures were frequently connected to human characteristics and attributes. The finesse of the fox, the reliability of the canine, and the beauty of the pony were viewed as impressions of human ethics and indecencies. These emblematic associations between creature conduct and human instinct allude to the persevering through interest with grasping the personalities of non-human creatures.

The Development of Ethology

The efficient logical investigation of creature conduct, known as ethology, is a generally present day discipline. It arose in the mid twentieth hundred years, owing a lot of its improvement to the noteworthy work of three powerful figures: Konrad Lorenz, Nikolaas Tinbergen, and Karl von Frisch. These trailblazers established the groundworks for the investigation of ethology and the investigation of creature conduct in a logical setting.

Konrad Lorenz: The Dad of Ethology

Konrad Lorenz, as examined in a past investigation, made critical commitments to the comprehension of creature conduct, engraving, and natural ways of behaving. His work with greylag geese and different species uncovered the complicated manners by which creatures associate with their current circumstance, convey, and adjust to make due. Lorenz's exploration stressed the significance of concentrating on creatures in their normal living spaces and figuring out a definitive and general reasons for their ways of behaving.

Nikolaas Tinbergen: The Investigation of Fixed Activity Examples

Nikolaas Tinbergen, a Dutch ethologist, presented the idea of fixed activity designs (FAPs) in creature conduct. FAPs are natural ways of behaving set off by unambiguous improvements and executed in a generalized and succession explicit way. Tinbergen's work underlined that these ways of behaving were designed into the science of creatures, molded by regular choice. He additionally made huge commitments to the comprehension of sense and the job of hereditary qualities in conduct.

Tinbergen's way to deal with the investigation of creature conduct included posing four key inquiries: the causation, ontogeny, capability, and development of a way of behaving. This structure gave a methodical approach to investigating and grasping the intricacies of creature conduct.

Karl von Frisch: Interpreting Creature Correspondence

Karl von Frisch, an Austrian ethologist, zeroed in on the investigation of creature correspondence, especially in honey bees. His work disentangled the unpredictable manners by which honey bees pass data about the area of nectar sources on to their hive mates through a remarkable dance language. Von Frisch's examination showed the intricacy of creature correspondence frameworks and uncovered that creatures could pass nitty gritty data about their current circumstance on to different individuals from their species.

The Job of Ethology in Figuring out Conduct

Ethology addresses a takeoff from conventional lab based examinations, as it looks to figure out the way of behaving of creatures in their regular environments. This approach is established in the conviction that creatures' ways of behaving have developed as versatile reactions to their particular environmental specialties.

Ethologists notice creatures in their regular habitats, observing their ways of behaving, specialized strategies, and communications with their environmental elements and conspecifics (individuals from similar species). These perceptions give basic experiences into how creatures adjust to their surroundings and the developmental explanations behind their ways of behaving.

Engraving and Natural Way of behaving

One of the critical bits of knowledge from ethology is the peculiarity of engraving, which was at first found by Konrad Lorenz. Engraving is a cycle through which youthful creatures structure solid and quick connections to the principal moving item they see, commonly their parent. This conduct guarantees that the youthful creatures get care and assurance from their guardians.

Engraving features the presence of natural ways of behaving — activities that creatures are brought into the world with and don't have to learn. These ways of behaving are hereditarily customized and are frequently basic for endurance and propagation. Understanding the job of natural ways of behaving in creatures' lives has significant ramifications for the investigation of conduct.

Correspondence and Social Designs

Ethologists additionally investigate the specialized strategies and social designs of different species. Creatures depend on various signs to pass data on to each other, like vocalizations, non-verbal communication, and substance signals. These correspondence frameworks assume a critical part in planning bunch exercises, mating, raising posterity, and safeguarding regions.

By concentrating on creature correspondence and social designs, ethologists gain bits of knowledge into the complicated collaborations and pecking orders inside creature social orders. For example, the romance ceremonies of birds, the predominance presentations of wolves, and the helpful rummaging procedures of insects all include complex correspondence and social ways of behaving that have advanced to streamline the endurance and propagation of the species.

Parental Consideration and Conceptive Techniques

One more area of interest for ethologists is the investigation of parental consideration and conceptive techniques. Various species utilize different techniques to guarantee the endurance of their posterity, from committed parental consideration to brood parasitism, where one animal groups lays its eggs in the home of another.

The investigation of parental consideration gives bits of knowledge into the penances and ways of behaving that creatures show to raise their young. Whether it's the sustaining care of warm blooded animals, the exact temperature guideline of reptile homes, or the provisioning of food by specific birds, these ways of behaving are molded by developmental tensions to improve the wellness of posterity.

The Importance of Creature Conduct

The investigation of creature conduct isn't restricted to the scholarly community; it has certifiable applications and extensive ramifications. It offers a significant comprehension of the mind boggling associations between every single living animal, rising above species limits. This information has down to earth and moral importance in different spaces.

Preservation and Biodiversity

Ethology assumes a critical part in protection endeavors, assisting scientists with figuring out the ways of behaving of jeopardized species and the effects of living space obliteration. By understanding how creatures act in their regular living spaces, researchers can distinguish the particular dangers these animals face and foster systems to secure and safeguard biodiversity.

Understanding creature ways of behaving additionally supports the renewed introduction of species into their regular living spaces, as it empowers preservationists to configuration discharge programs that think about the creatures' conduct needs and necessities for fruitful transformation.

Creature Government assistance and Cultivation

In the domain of animal government assistance and cultivation, the bits of knowledge acquired from ethological research advise the consideration and treatment regarding animals in different settings, like homesteads, zoos, and examination offices. Ethological studies have prompted the advancement of more altruistic and species-explicit practices for the lodging, taking care of, and enhancement of creatures in bondage.

Creature government assistance contemplations additionally stretch out to friend creatures. Understanding their ways of behaving and correspondence signals upgrades our capacity to give proper consideration and cultivate positive connections among people and creatures.

Human Culture and Brain science

The investigation of creature conduct has huge ramifications for how we might interpret human way of behaving and brain science. Ethological research uncovers matches between the ways of behaving of creatures and people, revealing insight into the transformative foundations of specific human qualities and ways of behaving.

Ethological bits of knowledge into subjects like social holding, collaboration, territoriality, and correspondence offer important points of view for grasping our own ways of behaving and cultural designs. These equals act as a wake up call of our place inside the more extensive setting of the normal world and our common developmental legacy with different species.

The Continuous Mission for Understanding

The investigation of creature conduct is a continuous excursion, with new disclosures ceaselessly growing our comprehension. Ethologists utilize cutting edge innovation, hereditary qualities, and neuroscience to dive further into the complexities of conduct, opening the neurological cycles and hereditary underpinnings that drive creature activities.

While much has been realized, there is still an incredible arrangement that stays obscure. The regular world is an immense and complex embroidery, and the investigation of creature conduct is a consistent journey for understanding. This mission welcomes us to get clarification on pressing issues, notice the world with an open-minded perspective, and value the miracles of the set of all animals.

In the expressions of Konrad Lorenz, one of the establishing figures of ethology, "We need to surrender the wonderful idea that each man, each human progress, has an option to the accomplishments of our science, our way of life. We need to start from the very beginning again toward the start and make individuals intrigued by the basic truth: we can comprehend what we know."

The journey for understanding creature conduct is a festival of the noteworthy variety of life on The planet. It is an affirmation of the getting through secret and excellence of the normal world, a world that coaxes us to investigate, learn, and interface with the complicated and entrancing personalities of non-human creatures.

4. **Purpose and Scope of the Book**

The reason for this book is to dig into the enamoring universe of creature conduct, revealing insight into the mind boggling and various manners by which non-human creatures explore their surroundings, impart, adjust, and flourish. We leave on an excursion to reveal the intricacies of the set of all animals, directed by the insight of trailblazers like Konrad Lorenz, while likewise investigating the more extensive ramifications of this information for how we might interpret the regular world and our place inside it.

The Reason for the Book

Praise the Magnificence and Intricacy of Creature Conduct: One of the main roles of this book is to commend the lavishness and variety of creature conduct. From the romance ceremonies of birds to the social elements of primates, we intend to feature the stunning transformations and ways of behaving that have advanced north of millions of years. By exhibiting the miracles of the set of all animals, we try to cultivate a profound appreciation for the regular world and its striking occupants.

Reveal the Instruments and Works: We dig into the components and capabilities behind different creature ways of behaving. From the perspective of Konrad Lorenz's work and the experiences of ethology, we plan to unwind the secrets of why creatures act the manner in which they do. We investigate a definitive and general reasons for ways of behaving, revealing insight into the transformative tensions and prompt triggers that drive creature activities.

Illuminate Protection and Natural Mindfulness: The book accentuates the importance of creature conduct to preservation and biological mindfulness. We feature the significance of understanding the jobs that various species play in their biological systems and the difficulties they face in an impacting world. By displaying the meaning of creature conduct in these specific circumstances, we expect to move a feeling of obligation toward the regular world and its protection.

Draw Equals with Human Way of behaving: Through the investigation of creature conduct, we draw matches with human way of behaving and society. We investigate the common transformative foundations of specific ways of behaving, like social holding, correspondence, and collaboration. By analyzing these equals, we welcome perusers to think about our place inside the more extensive setting of the regular world and the illustrations we can draw from the animals of the world collectively.

Encourage Interest and Appreciation: The book means to arouse interest in our general surroundings. We welcome perusers to clarify some pressing issues, notice the normal world with an open-minded perspective, and value the miracles of the animals of the world collectively. By cultivating a feeling of marvel and request, we desire to energize a more profound association with the regular world.

The Extent of the Book

The extent of this book is far reaching, including a large number of points connected with creature conduct. We investigate the accompanying key regions:

Correspondence in the Collective of animals: We dive into the different specialized strategies utilized by creatures, from vocalizations to non-verbal communication and synthetic signals. Our investigation features the mind boggling manners by which creatures pass on data about food sources, expected dangers, social orders, and that's just the beginning.

Territoriality and Social Designs: The book investigates the elements of regional conduct in the set of all animals, from the stamping and protection of domains to the foundation of social ordered progressions. We analyze how creatures participate in regional questions and coordinate inside gatherings.

Romance and Mating Ceremonies: We explore the intricate romance customs of creatures, from the mind boggling moves of birds to the presentations of fish and the calls of creatures of land and water. Our investigation reveals insight into the methodologies creatures utilize to draw in mates and guarantee the endurance of their posterity.

Parental Consideration and Conceptive Systems: The book digs into the devotion and methodologies utilized by guardians to raise their young. We investigate the variety of parental consideration in different species, from vertebrates to birds and bugs. By concentrating on parental consideration, we gain experiences into the penances and obligations of sustaining the future.

Lined up with Human Way of behaving: All through the book, we draw matches between creature conduct and human way of behaving, offering experiences into the common developmental starting points of specific qualities. We investigate how the investigation of the animals of the world collectively can educate our comprehension regarding human culture, brain science, and our relationship with the normal world.

Tradition of Konrad Lorenz: The getting through tradition of Konrad Lorenz, a trailblazer in the area of ethology, is a focal topic of the book. We feature his commitments to the investigation of creature conduct and his effect on the area of ethology. Lorenz's work fills in as a directing light in our investigation of the collective of animals.

The Crowd for the Book

This book is planned for a wide crowd, including:

Nature Devotees: Nature darlings, untamed life fans, and the individuals who value the excellence of the normal world will track down this book an enthralling investigation of creature conduct.

Understudies and Teachers: Understudies, instructors, and analysts in the areas of science, nature, and creature science will profit from the complete outline of creature conduct and its significance.

Moderates and Hippies: Those enthusiastic about preservation and ecological assurance will acquire bits of knowledge into the significance of figuring out creature conduct for biodiversity protection.

Inquisitive Perusers: Anybody with an oddity about the normal world, creature conduct, and the associations among human and non-human creatures will find this book drawing in and edifying.

Overall population: The book is written in a way open to the overall population, welcoming perusers, everything being equal, to leave on an excursion of revelation and appreciation.

Chapter 1

The Life and Work of Konrad Lorenz

Konrad Lorenz, perhaps of the most powerful figure in the area of ethology, was a researcher whose work everlastingly changed how we might interpret creature conduct. Brought into the world Austria, Lorenz's notable exploration and sharp experiences into the personalities and ways of behaving of non-human creatures have made a permanent imprint on the investigation of ethology, engraving, and the comprehension of natural ways of behaving. This investigation dives into the life and work of Konrad Lorenz, a man whose interest and enthusiasm for the normal world reshaped our view of the set of all animals.

Early Life and Impacts

Konrad Lorenz was naturally introduced to a family with a profound appreciation for nature and the outside. His dad, Heinrich Lorenz, was a conspicuous doctor, and his mom, Emma, shared his enthusiasm for the regular world. Experiencing childhood in this climate, Lorenz fostered an early interest with untamed life, particularly birds.

The youthful Lorenz's initial impacts were mixed and different. He drew motivation from crafted by Charles Darwin, Sigmund Freud, and different parts of the humanities, including writing and reasoning. This multidisciplinary approach would later turn into a sign of his work, as he coordinated his affection for craftsmanship, science, and the humanities into his examination.

Instructive Foundation

Lorenz's scholastic process took him to the College of Vienna, where he procured a physician certification in 1928. While his underlying examinations were in human medication, Lorenz's well established interest in the normal world persevered, ultimately driving him to seek after examinations in zoology. His obligation to the investigation of creatures resembled his scholastic interests in medication, denoting the start of a long lasting excursion committed to figuring out the mind boggling universe of creature conduct.

Engraving and Ethology

Lorenz's introduction to the investigation of creature conduct started with an interest for the ways of behaving of birds. During the 1930s, he led spearheading research on engraving, a peculiarity he initially portrayed. Engraving is the interaction by which youthful creatures structure solid and fast connections to the main moving article they see, ordinarily their parent. Lorenz's work with greylag geese showed the significant impact of early encounters on creature conduct.

Perhaps of his most well known try included a gathering of goslings that engraved on him, following him as though he were their mom. This cycle uncovered that the bond shaped among parent and posterity was not simply a consequence of maternal consideration but rather was profoundly imbued in the science and conduct of the creatures. Lorenz's experiences into engraving gave an establishment to understanding how creatures learn and adjust to their surroundings and how these ways of behaving have developed as techniques for endurance.

Fixed Activity Examples and Inborn Ways of behaving

One more key idea presented by Lorenz is that of fixed activity designs (FAPs). Fixed activity designs are natural ways of behaving that are set off by unambiguous upgrades and executed in a generalized and succession explicit way. These ways of behaving are normal for an animal varieties and are hereditarily customized. Lorenz's work stressed that FAPs were designed into the science of creatures and were formed by regular choice.

His examinations on the way of behaving of creatures like the stickleback fish and the graylag goose uncovered the presence of FAPs in their ways of behaving. For instance, the egg-recovery conduct of the graylag goose includes the intuitive demonstration of moving any uprooted egg once more into its home. This conduct is an illustration of a proper activity design, as it is designed and generalized.

Ethology as a Discipline

Lorenz's work established the groundwork for the area of ethology, the logical investigation of creature conduct. Ethology is portrayed by its attention on figuring out the way of behaving of creatures in their regular habitats. It stresses the significance of noticing creatures in their local territories to acquire a genuine comprehension of their ways of behaving.

During the twentieth hundred years, Lorenz, alongside other powerful figures in the field like Nikolaas Tinbergen, laid out the standards and strategies of ethology. They suggested that the way of behaving of creatures isn't arbitrary yet is well established in the developmental tensions looked by species over centuries.

Ethologists plan to study and figure out ways of behaving from both extreme and general viewpoints, investigating the developmental explanations behind conduct and the quick triggers or instruments that produce it.

Engraving and the Graylag Goose

Lorenz's work with the graylag goose was instrumental in molding how we might interpret engraving and natural ways of behaving. In his renowned trials, he exhibited that goslings engraved on the main moving item they saw, frequently Lorenz himself. This engraving system prompted the goslings following Lorenz as though he were their mom, showing the significant impact of early encounters on their way of behaving.

Lorenz's perceptions of engraving in graylag geese uncovered that the bond shaped among parent and posterity was profoundly imbued in the science and conduct of the creatures. It likewise featured that engraving is a basic versatile component that improves the endurance of the youthful.

The Correspondence of Creatures

Lorenz was additionally profoundly inspired by the correspondence of creatures, especially birds. He noticed the multifaceted vocalizations and non-verbal communication that creatures use to pass data on to each other. Lorenz's work on creature correspondence disclosed the perplexing manners by which creatures trade data and keep up with social designs.

One of his eminent investigations included jackdaws, a sort of crow. Lorenz found that jackdaws had explicit calls to declare the revelation of food, and different jackdaws would answer by running to the area. This correspondence component was imperative for their endurance, as it empowered them to participate in searching and safeguarding their region.

Lorenz's Imaginative and Abstract Impact

Notwithstanding his logical work, Lorenz had a profound appreciation for craftsmanship and writing, which essentially impacted his way to deal with concentrating on creature conduct. He was known for his creative delineations of creatures and their ways of behaving, integrating his affection for style into his logical work.

His capacity to pass the miracles of the animals of the world collectively on to an overall crowd was a demonstration of his scholarly gifts. Lorenz's well known works and talks added to a developing familiarity with the magnificence and intricacy of the creature world, overcoming any issues between the logical investigation of creature conduct and the more extensive public's enthusiasm for nature.

Moral and Philosophical Ramifications

Lorenz's work and the area of ethology have brought up significant moral and philosophical issues in regards to our relationship with the animals of the world collectively. The acknowledgment of intrinsic ways of behaving and the organic underpinnings of creature conduct challenge customary human-centric perspectives that accentuate human excellence.

Lorenz's work features the interconnectedness of every living being and the intricacy and extravagance of the creature world. Ethology has prodded conversations on creature government assistance, morals, and our obligations as stewards of the normal world.

Heritage and Impact

Konrad Lorenz's work significantly affected how we might interpret creature conduct and its part in the regular world. His examination uncovered that creature conduct isn't erratic however is well established in development and variation. His experiences into engraving, natural way of behaving, and correspondence gave a system to understanding the mind boggling ways of behaving displayed by creatures in their regular territories.

Lorenz's heritage keeps on impacting the investigation of creature conduct, preservation endeavors, and our philosophical comprehension of the spot of people in the normal world. His work fills in as a demonstration of the force of interest and perception in disentangling the secrets of the collective of animals.

Present day Ethology

The area of ethology has proceeded to develop and prosper right after Lorenz's spearheading work. Present day ethologists expand upon his central thoughts, integrating trend setting innovations, for example, video recording, hereditary investigation, and neuroscience to dive much more profound into the secrets of creature conduct.

This multidisciplinary approach has empowered analysts to unwind the brain components that underlie conduct, examine the hereditary premise of specific ways of behaving, and investigate the effects of ecological changes on creature populaces. Ethology plays had a pivotal impact in preservation endeavors, as specialists apply how they might interpret creature conduct to safeguard jeopardized species and protect biodiversity.

1.1 Early Life and Influences

The early life and impacts of an individual can shape the course of their whole presence. From family and cultural elements to instructive encounters and social foundation, these variables assume a significant part in molding an individual's qualities, convictions, and yearnings. In this paper, we will investigate the early life and impacts of an individual, taking into account the different components that add to their turn of events and at last characterize who they become.

Family and Childhood

Family is in many cases the most compelling component of a person's initial life. It is inside the family that one initially finds out about affection, trust, and the principal esteems that will direct them all through their life. The nuclear family gives an establishment to an individual's healthy identity, how they might interpret connections, and their perspective.

Guardians are the essential powerhouses in a kid's life. Their convictions, values, and ways of behaving are noticed and consumed by their youngsters, frequently without cognizant mindfulness. Nurturing styles can differ essentially, going from definitive to lenient, and each approach can particularly affect a kid's turn of events.

For example, youngsters raised by tyrant guardians might grow up with major areas of strength for an of discipline and regard for power however may likewise battle with issues connected with independence and self-articulation. Then again, youngsters raised by lenient guardians might foster a more loosened up way to deal with rules and limits, possibly prompting hardships in self-guideline.

Kin likewise assume a urgent part in shaping a person's initial life. They are in many cases the primary friends and sidekicks an individual has, and their communications can affect social turn of events and the capacity to explore connections. Kin elements can change extraordinarily, from close obligations of help and fellowship to contentions and clashes that impact one's feeling of rivalry and participation.

Social Foundation

Social foundation is another huge element that shapes a person's initial life. Culture incorporates a large number of components, including language, customs, customs, and strict convictions. It characterizes how an individual sees the world, connects with others, and structures their personality.

For instance, a youngster experiencing childhood in a multicultural, cosmopolitan city might have openness to a rich embroidery of societies and perspectives, encouraging a feeling of transparency and variety. Conversely, a kid brought up in a more homogeneous social climate might foster a more grounded connection to their own way of life and might be less presented to elective points of view.

The social foundation additionally impacts a singular's qualities and standards. For example, a few societies focus on cooperation and local area, while others underline independence and individual achievement. These qualities can significantly influence a singular's needs and choices as they develop and develop.

Training and Learning

Training is a basic part of a person's initial life that can lastingly affect their future. The sort of schooling an individual gets, the nature of the foundations they join in, and their admittance to assets all assume a part in forming their insight, abilities, and valuable open doors.

Youth training, specifically, is instrumental in mental and social turn of events. It gives the establishment to education, numeracy, and interactive abilities. The nature of early instruction projects can change generally, and youngsters from various financial foundations might have inconsistent admittance to great instructive open doors.

The style of instruction and the educational plan likewise impact a person's perspective. For example, an understudy going to a strict school might be presented to a particular arrangement of strict convictions and values, which can significantly affect their otherworldly and moral turn of events. On the other hand, an understudy going to a common school might get more secularized instruction that underscores decisive reasoning and a more extensive scope of points of view.

Peer Connections

As people develop, peer connections become progressively significant. Kinships and social collaborations with peers assume a huge part in molding one's feeling of personality and having a place. Peer bunches offer open doors for socialization, support, and the investigation of shared interests.

Peer strain can be a strong impact in a singular's life. Teenagers, specifically, may feel strain to adjust to the standards and upsides of their friend bunch. This can prompt both positive and adverse results. Positive companion tension can support solid ways of behaving and esteems, while negative friend strain might prompt hazardous ways of behaving or adjustment to negative accepted practices.

Local area and Cultural Impacts

The more extensive local area and society wherein an individual is raised likewise assume an essential part in their initial life. Networks give amazing open doors to social commitment, sporting exercises, and openness to various social and financial gatherings. The idea of a local area can impact a singular's feeling that everything is safe and secure, having a place, and metro commitment.

Cultural elements, like financial circumstances and political environment, can affect a person's initial life in critical ways. Financial inconsistencies, for instance, can impact a singular's admittance to assets, amazing open doors, and the nature of their schooling. Political shakiness or social distress can establish a climate of vulnerability and dread, which can influence a singular's feeling of safety and prosperity.

Media and Innovation

In the present advanced age, media and innovation have become unmistakable impacts on a person's initial life. TV, the web, and virtual entertainment stages give admittance to an immense range of data and viewpoints. They can shape a singular's qualities, convictions, and goals, frequently without their full mindfulness.

Media can both reflect and shape cultural standards and values. TV programs, films, and online substance frequently depict specific ways of life, magnificence principles, and cultural standards. These portrayals can impact a singular's confidence, self-perception, and life objectives.

The web and online entertainment have additionally changed how people associate and communicate. They give valuable open doors to self-articulation, long range interpersonal communication, and admittance to data. In any case, they can likewise open people to cyberbullying, online badgering, and over the top screen time, which can adversely affect emotional well-being and social turn of events.

Good examples and Powerful Figures

All through their initial life, people frequently experience good examples and powerful figures who can influence their desires and values. These good examples can be relatives, instructors, tutors, or people of note. The characteristics and accomplishments of these figures can move people and shape their desires.

For instance, a small kid might admire a parent who is an effective business visionary, seeking to emulate their example. A secondary school understudy might have an instructor who touches off their enthusiasm for a specific subject, impacting their decision of school major and vocation way. People of note, like researchers, competitors, specialists, and political pioneers, can likewise act as good examples, exhibiting the potential outcomes of progress and the qualities worth seeking after.

1.2 Evolution of Lorenz's Theories

The area of meteorology and confusion hypothesis owes a lot to the spearheading work of Edward N. Lorenz, an American mathematician and meteorologist who fundamentally added to how we might interpret weather conditions, the air, and the idea of confusion. Lorenz's excursion in the realm of science was set apart by progressive revelations and significant changes in how we might interpret complex frameworks. In this article, we will investigate the development of Lorenz's hypotheses and their effect on different logical disciplines.

Early Life and Instruction

Edward Norton Lorenz was brought into the world on May 23, 1917, in West Hartford, Connecticut. His initial scholarly interests were basically in math, and he procured a four year certification in math from Dartmouth School in 1938. Subsequent to functioning as a logarithmic topologist for a couple of years, Lorenz chose to move his concentration to meteorology and got a graduate degree in the subject from the Massachusetts Organization of Innovation (MIT) in 1943.

Lorenz's choice to change from unadulterated arithmetic to meteorology was affected by his acknowledgment of the difficult and unknown nature of climate expectation. Meteorology was a field that charmed him because of its true capacity for perplexing, nonlinear way of behaving, which math had not yet enough tended to.

The Revelation of Deterministic Mayhem

In the mid 1960s, while dealing with mathematical climate forecast at the Massachusetts Establishment of Innovation, Lorenz made a pivotal revelation that would steer disarray hypothesis. He was utilizing a PC to recreate and foresee weather conditions when he saw something startling. He ran a weather conditions model with a minor change in one of the underlying circumstances, identical to modifying the info information just barely.

Lorenz anticipated that the model should deliver an outcome that firmly looked like the first run. Nonetheless, what he found was totally unforeseen. The two reproductions, in spite of their minor uniqueness in input, created decisively unique long haul atmospheric conditions. This disclosure prompted the now-well known representation of the "butterfly impact." Lorenz presumed that little changes in beginning circumstances could prompt tremendously various results, suggesting an essential unusualness in weather conditions guaging.

Lorenz's work on this idea was distributed in an original paper named "Deterministic Nonperiodic Stream" in the Diary of the Air Sciences in 1963. In this paper, Lorenz represented how delicate reliance on starting circumstances could prompt tumultuous conduct in powerful frameworks, an idea that later became known as the "Lorenz attractor." This revelation changed how we might interpret complex frameworks and established the groundwork for disorder hypothesis.

Influence on Meteorology

Lorenz's momentous work on deterministic mayhem significantly affected the area of meteorology. Preceding his disclosures, weather conditions models basically depended on direct, deterministic conditions that expected the air acted typically. Lorenz's disclosure broke this suspicion, stressing the inborn eccentricism of climate frameworks.

Meteorologists started to perceive that drawn out weather conditions gauges were restricted in exactness because of the turbulent idea of the climate. This prompted a change in meteorological examination and estimating rehearses. Rather than making progress toward steadily protracting gauge skylines, meteorologists zeroed in on momentary forecasts and working on the comprehension of climatic cycles.

The presentation of turmoil hypothesis into meteorology additionally propelled the advancement of mathematical climate expectation models that consolidated stochastic components, perceiving the inborn impediments in deterministic methodologies. These models consider probabilistic estimates and assist meteorologists with better conveying the vulnerability related with climate expectations.

Interdisciplinary Impact

Lorenz's work reached out a long ways past the area of meteorology. His disclosure of deterministic tumult impacted different logical disciplines and areas of study.

Material science: Turmoil hypothesis tracked down its direction into physical science, particularly in the investigation of nonlinear dynamical frameworks. It tested the Newtonian thought that the universe worked typically and directly. Physicists started to investigate mayhem in a large number of peculiarities, from the way of behaving of liquids to the elements of particles in non-direct frameworks.

Arithmetic: Lorenz's work added to the improvement of new numerical devices and ideas to grasp turbulent frameworks. This prompted propels in the investigation of fractals, bizarre attractors, and the topological properties of tumultuous frameworks.

Designing: Tumult hypothesis found applications in designing, especially in fields like control hypothesis and electrical circuits. Engineers perceived the significance of understanding and overseeing turbulent conduct in different frameworks and gadgets.

Financial matters: Mayhem hypothesis impacted monetary displaying and the comprehension of intricate monetary frameworks. Business analysts started to consolidate turbulent elements in their models to make sense of market conduct and monetary emergencies.

Science: Disorder hypothesis likewise advanced into science, especially in the investigation of biological frameworks and populace elements. Scientists understood that tumultuous vacillations could altogether affect biological systems.

Later Commitments and Respects

All through his vocation, Lorenz kept on making huge commitments to meteorology and tumult hypothesis. He created improved on numerical models to depict environmental convection and investigated the elements of mid-scope climate frameworks. His work on the "Lorenz Model" showed the way that straightforward frameworks could display tumultuous way of behaving, further outlining the boundless pertinence of turmoil hypothesis.

Lorenz's commitments didn't be ignored by mainstream researchers. He got various honors and respects, including the Carl-Gustaf Rossby Exploration Decoration from the American Meteorological Society, the Kyoto Prize, and the Crafoord Prize from the Regal Swedish Foundation of Sciences. These honors perceived his significant effect on the area of meteorology and complex frameworks.

1.3 Ethology and Its Impact on the Study of Animal Behavior

Ethology, the logical investigation of creature conduct, plays had a urgent impact in how we might interpret how creatures cooperate with their current circumstance, convey, and adjust to various circumstances. The field has developed throughout the long term, consolidating different philosophies and hypothetical systems, and essentially affects our insight into creatures as well as the human species. In this article, we will investigate the set of experiences, key ideas, philosophies, and the more extensive effect of ethology on the investigation of creature conduct.

Authentic Improvement of Ethology

Ethology as a particular logical discipline has its foundations in the mid twentieth 100 years, and it arose as a response to additional robotic and reductionist ways to deal with concentrating on creature conduct.

While behaviorism was common in brain science and creature research at that point, ethologists tried to grasp conduct with regards to the creature's regular habitat, its transformative history, and its versatile capabilities.

One of the pioneers behind ethology was Konrad Lorenz, an Austrian zoologist, who led broad exploration on the way of behaving of birds, especially engraving in waterfowl. Lorenz is credited with fostering the idea of intrinsic delivering components (IRM) and fixed activity designs (FAPs), which are untaught, generalized ways of behaving set off by unambiguous key boosts. Lorenz's work, alongside that of Nikolaas Tinbergen, one more spearheading ethologist, established the groundwork for the investigation of creature conduct according to a transformative viewpoint.

Key Ideas in Ethology

Inborn Way of behaving: Ethologists underscore the meaning of intrinsic ways of behaving, which are ways of behaving that are hereditarily modified and don't need learning. These ways of behaving are believed to be molded by normal determination and are fundamental for a creature's endurance and proliferation.

Fixed Activity Examples (FAPs): FAPs are generalized, exceptionally unsurprising arrangements of ways of behaving set off by unambiguous boosts. When started, these ways of behaving are normally finished without outer impedance. FAPs are viewed as versatile reactions to explicit ecological signals.

Sign Upgrades: Ethologists are especially inspired by the boosts or signals that trigger explicit ways of behaving. These sign improvements, otherwise called releasers, are many times exceptionally unambiguous and can incorporate visual, hear-able, or compound prompts.

Engraving: Engraving is a basic idea in ethology, as exhibited by Konrad Lorenz's work. It alludes to a delicate period from the get-go in a creature's life during which they structure solid connections to explicit items or people. This peculiarity is frequently basic for the endurance of precocial species.

Fixed Activity Examples: These are untaught, instinctual ways of behaving that are set off by unambiguous upgrades. For instance, the home structure conduct of birds or the web-turning conduct of bugs.

Intrinsic Delivering Instruments (IRM): These are brain systems that perceive explicit sign upgrades and trigger the suitable fixed activity design. IRMs are designed into a creature's sensory system.

Ideal Scavenging Hypothesis: This hypothesis investigates how creatures settle on conclusions about how to designate their significant investment to boost their food admission while limiting the dangers and expenses related with searching.

Philosophies in Ethology

Ethologists utilize different strategies to concentrate on creature conduct, with an emphasis on noticing creatures in their regular habitats and under controlled conditions. A portion of the key systems include:

Field Perceptions: Noticing creatures in their normal environments permits ethologists to concentrate on conduct as it happens with regards to a creature's everyday existence. This approach frequently includes expanded times of perception and information assortment.

Trial Studies: Ethologists likewise lead controlled analyses to research explicit parts of creature conduct. These tests might include controlling ecological upgrades or noticing conduct in a controlled setting.

Relative Investigations: Ethologists frequently contrast conduct across various species with grasp the advancement of explicit ways of behaving or variations. Such examinations give experiences into the connections among conduct and natural or transformative variables.

Long haul Exploration: A few ethologists take part in long haul research, following the way of behaving of people or populaces overstretched periods. This considers the investigation of life narratives, conceptive techniques, and the effect of ecological changes.

Influence on the Investigation of Creature Conduct

Ethology significantly affects the investigation of creature conduct in more than one way:

Shift Towards a Naturalistic Viewpoint: Ethology underscored the significance of concentrating on conduct with regards to a creature's indigenous habitat. This shift away from controlled lab settings has permitted scientists to acquire a more all encompassing comprehension of creature conduct.

Acknowledgment of Natural Way of behaving: Ethologists assumed a key part in featuring the meaning of inborn way of behaving and the possibility that specific ways of behaving are designed and have developed over the long run because of their versatile worth.

Transformative Viewpoint: Ethology has added to the comprehension of conduct from a developmental outlook. The investigation of fixed activity designs, sign boosts, and the job of ways of behaving in endurance and multiplication has revealed insight into the transformative cycles shaping way of behaving.

Applications in Preservation Science: Ethological research has significant ramifications for protection endeavors. Understanding the normal ways of behaving and biological requirements of species is basic for powerful protection and the board.

Cross-Species Correlations: Ethologists have led near examinations that assist with uncovering the shared characteristics and varieties in conduct across species. This has prompted experiences into the common transformative history of specific ways of behaving.

Interdisciplinary Coordinated efforts: Ethology has empowered joint efforts between scientists, biologists, analysts, and different fields. Scientists from different foundations add to a more extensive comprehension of creature conduct.

Moral Contemplations: Ethologists have added to conversations on creature government assistance and moral treatment, featuring the significance of thinking about the normal ways of behaving and needs of creatures in imprisonment.

Broadened Impact on the Investigation of Human Way of behaving

While ethology principally centers around non-human creature conduct, its standards and procedures have likewise impacted the investigation of human way of behaving. Relative brain science, for instance, attracts on ethological ways to deal with grasp the transformative underlying foundations of human ways of behaving and mental cycles.

Also, parts of human brain research, like connection hypothesis, have been educated by ethological ideas. Connection hypothesis, as evolved by John Bowlby, accentuates the significance of early close to home connections among youngsters and their parental figures, like the idea of engraving in creatures.

Moreover, ethological research broadly affects the sociologies by testing the short-sighted behaviorist perspective on people as clean slate (clean canvases) and underscoring the job of transformative and hereditary elements in shaping human way of behaving.

1.4Key Contributions and Research Methods

Brain science, as a logical discipline, has a rich history set apart by various key commitments and different exploration techniques. These commitments have molded the field and our comprehension of human way of behaving, cognizance, and feelings. In this exposition, we will investigate probably the main commitments and the different exploration techniques utilized in brain science, featuring how they have progressed the field.

Structuralism and Functionalism:

Structuralism, established by Wilhelm Wundt in the late nineteenth 100 years, expected to dissect the fundamental components of cognizance. Wundt's accentuation on thoughtfulness as a strategy for understanding mental cycles laid the foundation for the investigation of human discernment.

Functionalism, advocated by William James, moved the concentration from investigating mental designs to inspecting the elements of cognizance. It featured the versatile idea of mental cycles and their part in assisting people with adjusting to their current circumstance.

Behaviorism:

John B. Watson and B.F. Skinner drove the behaviorist development, which overwhelmed brain science in the mid twentieth 100 years. Behaviorism stressed the investigation of detectable ways of behaving and the impact of natural elements on conduct. This approach added to the improvement of change in behavior patterns treatments and learning speculations.

Mental Transformation:

The mental unrest, which arose during the twentieth 100 years, denoted a shift away from behaviorism. Analysts like Ulric Neisser and George Mill operator supported for the investigation of mental cycles and mental designs. This development prompted the improvement of mental brain science, which investigates points, for example, memory, critical thinking, and navigation.

Therapy:

Sigmund Freud's psychoanalytic hypothesis has impacted brain science and psychotherapy. Freud's work on the oblivious brain, guard systems, and the job of youth encounters in molding character has formed the field of clinical brain science and the comprehension of the human mind.

Humanistic Brain science:

Humanistic brain science, spearheaded by Abraham Maslow and Carl Rogers, underscores the significance of individual development, self-realization, and the quest for individual importance. This approach has added to the improvement of humanistic treatments and positive brain research.

Natural Brain research:

Analysts like Paul Broca and Carl Wernicke made huge commitments to grasping the organic premise of conduct, especially through their work on the mind and language. This established the groundwork for the subfield of neuropsychology and the investigation of mind conduct connections.

Developmental Brain science:

Developmental brain science, drove by figures like Leda Cosmides and John Tooby, applies standards of transformative hypothesis to grasp human way of behaving. This point of view investigates how our developmental history has formed our mental, close to home, and social cycles.

Multifaceted Brain research:

Geert Hofstede made significant commitments to multifaceted brain research by fostering a model for grasping social aspects and their effect on human way of behaving. His work has expanded how we might interpret social variety and its suggestions for brain research.

Social Brain science:

Kurt Lewin is much of the time viewed as one of the originators behind friendly brain research. His examination on overall vibes, administration, and social impact fundamentally added to the comprehension of what people are meant for by their social climate.

Formative Brain research:

Jean Piaget's work in formative brain research reformed how we might interpret mental improvement in kids. His phases of mental turn of events, like the sensorimotor and concrete functional stages, are key to the field.

Research Techniques in Brain science

Brain science utilizes an extensive variety of examination strategies to explore human way of behaving and mental cycles. These strategies can be extensively sorted into the accompanying:

Test Technique:

Tests include controlling at least one factors to notice their consequences for conduct or mental cycles. Trial research considers the foundation of circumstances and logical results connections. Analysts control factors and frequently utilize arbitrary task to make exploratory and control gatherings. This strategy is especially predominant in mental and trial brain research.

Observational Technique:

Observational examinations include watching and keep conduct in a naturalistic setting with practically no trial control. Analysts might utilize organized or unstructured perceptions. This technique is normally utilized in regions like formative brain science and social brain science.

Reviews and Surveys:

Reviews and surveys are utilized to gather information through self-announcing. They are utilized in different parts of brain science to assemble data on perspectives, convictions, and ways of behaving. This strategy is savvy yet might be dependent upon reaction predisposition.

Contextual analyses:

Contextual analyses include top to bottom assessments of individual subjects or little gatherings. They give itemized experiences into explicit cases however are restricted in their capacity to sum up discoveries to a more extensive populace. Clinical brain science frequently uses contextual analyses.

Correlational Investigations:

Correlational investigations analyze the connection between at least two factors without control. Analysts ascertain connection coefficients to survey the strength and heading of affiliations. Correlational exploration is generally utilized in fields like instructive brain science and wellbeing brain research.

Longitudinal Investigations:

Longitudinal investigations include following similar gathering of people or subjects over a drawn out period. This technique is especially valuable for contemplating formative endlessly changes after some time in regions like life expectancy brain science.

Cross-Sectional Examinations:

Cross-sectional examinations include the concurrent investigation of people of various age gatherings or at various moments. They are valuable for contrasting various gatherings and concentrating on age-related contrasts in regions like geropsychology.

Neuroimaging and Psychophysiological Measures:

Neuroimaging strategies, like fMRI and EEG, permit specialists to concentrate on the cerebrum's action and design. Psychophysiological measures, similar to pulse and skin conductance, furnish experiences into physiological reactions related with mental states and feelings.

Content Examination:

Content examination includes efficiently breaking down the substance of composed, verbal, or visual correspondence. It is utilized in regions like media brain research to analyze subjects, messages, and portrayals in different media structures.

Creature Exploration:

Creature research, especially in relative brain science and social neuroscience, includes concentrating on creature conduct to acquire bits of knowledge into human way of behaving. This examination might incorporate controlled tests, observational investigations, and the control of factors.

Moral Contemplations in Mental Exploration

The area of brain science puts serious areas of strength for an on moral contemplations in research. Moral rules are intended to safeguard the government assistance and freedoms of exploration members. Key moral standards incorporate getting educated assent, keeping up with privacy, limiting damage, and guaranteeing that examination is directed with respectability and straightforwardness. Moral rules have been created by proficient associations like the American Mental Affiliation (APA) to guarantee that examination is directed capably and morally.

Chapter 2

Nature vs. Nurture: The Debate Continues

The nature versus sustain banter has been a focal and getting through question in the area of brain research for a really long time. It spins around the overall impact of hereditary variables (nature) and ecological elements (sustain) on different parts of human turn of events and conduct. This discussion has started broad exploration, conversation, and debate inside the field, as researchers and researchers look to figure out the transaction among hereditary qualities and climate in molding what our identity is. In this article, we will dig into the historical backdrop of the nature versus support banter, look at key parts of human turn of events and conduct, and investigate the contemporary comprehension of this mind boggling and complex issue.

Authentic Starting points of the Discussion

The nature versus sustain banter has antiquated roots, with rationalists and scholars contemplating the starting points of human characteristics and conduct for quite a long time. Plato and Aristotle, for instance, participated in conversations about whether information was inborn (nature) or gained through experience (sustain). This discussion went on through the ages and tracked down reverberation in different spaces, including reasoning, brain research, and science.

It was during the nineteenth and twentieth hundreds of years that the discussion acquired noticeable quality in the arising area of brain research. Prominent figures like Sir Francis Galton, a cousin of Charles Darwin, supported the meaning of heredity and upheld for the legacy of scholarly capacities and character qualities. On the opposite side of the discussion, behaviorist scholars like John B. Watson stressed the job of climate and learning in significantly shaping human way of behaving, excusing the significance of heredity.

Key Parts of the Discussion

The nature versus sustain banter envelops different parts of human turn of events and conduct, including knowledge, character, mental problems, and that's only the tip of the iceberg. We should investigate these critical viewpoints to all the more likely figure out the idea of the discussion.

Insight:

Knowledge has been a focal subject in the nature versus support banter. Early advocates of the hereditarian view, for example, Galton, accepted that knowledge had solid hereditary roots. Notwithstanding, contemporary exploration recommends that both hereditary and natural elements assume a part in deciding a singular's knowledge. Twin and reception studies have been critical in this exploration, uncovering that both hereditary qualities and childhood add to a person's mental capacities.

Character:

Character qualities, like extraversion, reliability, and neuroticism, have been investigated with regards to the nature versus sustain banter. Analysts have directed twin and family studies to grasp the hereditary and natural effects on character. While hereditary qualities might give an inclination to specific characteristics, ecological variables, for example, nurturing and valuable encounters, likewise essentially add to character improvement.

Mental Problems:

The etiology of mental problems is an intricate issue inside the nature versus support banter. Conditions like schizophrenia, bipolar turmoil, and sadness are remembered to have both hereditary and ecological parts. Twin and family studies have shown that a hereditary inclination, joined with natural stressors, may build the gamble of fostering these problems.

Hostility and Savagery:

The discussion has stretched out to the investigation of forceful way of behaving and savagery. Analysts play analyzed the part of hereditary qualities in inclining people toward forceful propensities, while additionally recognizing the critical effect of ecological variables, like openness to savagery and adolescence injury.

Language Securing:

The discussion likewise addresses language advancement. While Noam Chomsky's hypothesis of general punctuation recommends a natural limit with respect to language, the significance of early semantic openness and ecological help is clear in kids' language securing.

Actual Attributes:

Actual characteristics, for example, level, eye tone, and certain medical issue, still up in the air by hereditary qualities. Notwithstanding, sustenance, wellbeing, and ecological variables can impact actual turn of events and the outflow of hereditary attributes.

The Job of Hereditary qualities

In the nature versus sustain banter, the hereditary part, frequently alluded to as "nature," assumes a pivotal part. Hereditary qualities includes the investigation of a singular's qualities or DNA, which convey guidelines for different physical and conduct characteristics. A few central issues with respect to hereditary qualities include:

Heredity: Hereditary data is passed starting with one age then onto the next through the course of multiplication. Kids acquire a blend of qualities from their folks, adding to their hereditary cosmetics.

Hereditary Variety: Hereditary variety happens through the recombination of qualities during sexual generation. This variety represents the variety of physical and social attributes saw in the human populace.

Hereditary Inclination: Hereditary elements can make an inclination for specific qualities or conditions. In any case, having a hereditary inclination doesn't ensure the statement of a particular characteristic or condition; it cooperates with natural variables.

Hereditary Exploration: Advances in hereditary qualities, for example, the Human Genome Undertaking, have given important bits of knowledge into the job of explicit qualities in different parts of human turn of events and conduct. Hereditary examination has added to how we might interpret innate circumstances and inclinations.

The Job of Climate

The natural part, frequently alluded to as "sustain," includes all outside factors that impact human turn of events and conduct. Central issues about the natural impact include:

Natural Factors: The climate incorporates different components, like family, culture, peers, schooling, financial status, nourishment, and encounters. These variables can shape a singular's turn of events and conduct.

Early Experience: Early encounters, particularly during basic times of improvement, can lastingly affect a person. Early supporting, connection, and mental feeling can impact mental and close to home turn of events.

Ecological Determinism: A few natural variables are deterministic, meaning they straightforwardly impact conduct or results. For instance, openness to lead harming can prompt mental impedances, showing the immediate impact of the climate.

Quality Climate Cooperation: The exchange among qualities and the climate is a key idea. Qualities can collaborate with ecological variables to impact conduct. For instance, people with a hereditary inclination to liquor abuse might be more powerless to the improvement of the condition in a climate with elevated degrees of liquor utilization.

The Contemporary Getting it

Contemporary brain science perceives that the nature versus sustain banter doesn't involve either/or however a perplexing transaction among hereditary qualities and the climate. Our comprehension has developed to think about quality climate cooperations, epigenetics, and the bidirectional connection among nature and sustain. A few vital improvements in the contemporary comprehension of the discussion include:

Epigenetics:

Epigenetics investigates how natural elements can impact the declaration of qualities. It includes synthetic changes to the DNA that can be given to ensuing ages. This idea highlights the powerful idea of quality climate collaborations.

Quality Climate Collaboration:

Scientists presently underline the cooperation among qualities and the climate. The two elements can impact each other in a proportional way. For instance, a person's hereditary cosmetics might impact their selection of conditions, which thus shapes their turn of events and conduct.

Versatility and Flexibility:

The human cerebrum displays a serious level of versatility, meaning it can adjust and revamp itself in light of encounters and ecological impacts. This versatility takes into consideration the possibility to conquer hereditary inclinations or early unfriendly encounters through certain ecological changes.

Individual Contrasts:

Perceiving that people shift in their hereditary cosmetics and natural encounters, contemporary brain science accentuates the investigation of individual contrasts. These distinctions are molded by novel blends of nature and sustain.

Transgenerational Impacts:

Research in transgenerational impacts centers around what natural encounters can mean for the person as well as people in the future through epigenetic adjustments. For instance, maternal pressure during pregnancy can affect the kid's turn of events.

Social and Relevant Contemplations:

Contemporary brain science recognizes the job of culture and setting in forming human turn of events and conduct. Social standards, values, and practices impact how people interface with their current circumstance and express their hereditary characteristics.

Intercession and Treatment:

In clinical brain science, mediations and medicines frequently center around adjusting ecological variables to reduce side effects or address conduct issues. This mirrors the comprehension that natural changes can impact a singular's prosperity and emotional wellness.

Instances of Quality Climate Communications

To delineate the mind boggling interchange among qualities and the climate, how about we think about a few explicit models:

Quality Climate Connection in Emotional wellness:

An individual might convey a hereditary inclination for sadness. In any case, the outflow of this inclination might rely upon ecological variables, like openness to ongoing pressure, injury, or antagonistic youth encounters. The collaboration between the hereditary inclination and natural stressors can expand the gamble of creating discouragement.

Qualities and Nourishment:

Hereditary varieties can impact a singular's reaction to dietary parts. For instance, certain individuals might have a hereditary inclination that makes them more delicate with the impacts of high-fat eating regimens, possibly prompting weight gain and related medical problems. The association among hereditary qualities and diet features the job of both nature and sustain in forming wellbeing results.

Instructive Accomplishment:

Research proposes that hereditary variables can add to a singular's scholarly capacities. In any case, the nature of instructive open doors and the help given by guardians and educators assume a significant part in scholastic achievement. The cooperation among hereditary qualities and the instructive climate impacts an individual's learning and accomplishment.

Social Impacts on Conduct:

Culture shapes different parts of conduct and personality. Hereditary attributes, for example, actual appearance or defenselessness to specific ailments, can be capable distinctively relying upon the social setting. For instance, the impression of excellence might shift across societies, affecting people's confidence and conduct.

The Ramifications of the Discussion

The nature versus sustain banter has significant ramifications for different fields and parts of society:

Instruction:

Understanding the interchange among hereditary qualities and climate is critical for teachers. It accentuates the significance of customized learning approaches that think about individual contrasts and offer help for understudies with assorted needs.

Clinical Brain science and Psychological wellness:

In the field of emotional wellness, perceiving quality climate connections is basic for diagnosing and treating conditions like uneasiness, sadness, and habit. Intercessions frequently center around both hereditary and natural elements.

Law enforcement:

The discussion has suggestions for the law enforcement framework, especially in figuring out the starting points of criminal way of behaving. Perceiving the job of both hereditary inclinations and unfriendly conditions can illuminate recovery endeavors and intercessions.

Nurturing and Kid Improvement:

Guardians assume a huge part in molding their youngsters' surroundings. Understanding the transaction among hereditary qualities and the climate can direct nurturing practices and mediations for youngster improvement.

General Wellbeing:

General wellbeing endeavors frequently plan to address natural factors that influence wellbeing results. Notwithstanding, an acknowledgment of quality climate communications can prompt more customized ways to deal with wellbeing advancement and illness counteraction.

Moral Contemplations

The nature versus sustain banter likewise raises moral contemplations, especially with regards to issues connected with hereditary testing and intercession. A few moral contemplations include:

Hereditary Testing and Protection:

As hereditary testing turns out to be more open, people face choices about whether to go through hereditary testing for different purposes, for example, wellbeing evaluation or lineage research. Guaranteeing the protection and secrecy of hereditary data is a basic moral concern.

Belittling:

The information on hereditary inclinations might prompt demonization or segregation. This is especially significant with regards to emotional well-being, as people with specific hereditary gamble elements might confront social bias.

Regenerative Decisions:

Hereditary data can impact regenerative choices, for example, family arranging and pre-birth testing. Moral inquiries emerge in regards to the utilization of hereditary data to choose or alter qualities in posterity.

Mediations and Upgrade:

The potential for hereditary intercessions, like quality altering or improvement, brings up moral issues about the limits of changing human instinct and the potential for unseen side-effects.

Contemporary Exploration and Future Bearings

Contemporary examination in brain science keeps on investigating the transaction among hereditary qualities and the climate. Propels in hereditary qualities, epigenetics, neuroscience, and conduct sciences give new bits of knowledge into the intricacies of the discussion.

Vast Affiliation Studies (GWAS):

GWAS have distinguished explicit hereditary varieties related with different characteristics and conditions. These examinations expect to reveal the hereditary premise of mind boggling characteristics, revealing insight into the job of hereditary qualities in conduct and illness.

Epigenetics:

Epigenetic research investigates how natural elements can alter quality articulation. Understanding epigenetic instruments adds to how we might interpret how the climate connects with qualities.

Quality Climate Connection Studies:

Analysts direct examinations that look at how hereditary elements and ecological openings interface to impact human way of behaving and wellbeing results. These investigations assist us with better grasping the subtleties of the nature versus support banter.

Neuroscience:

Progresses in neuroscience have prompted a more profound comprehension of how the mind answers ecological improvements. This examination features the brain components through which nature and sustain communicate to significantly mold conduct.

Social and Multifaceted Brain science:

Research in social and culturally diverse brain science investigates what culture means for conduct and character. It examines the complicated exchange between social standards, hereditary qualities, and ecological variables.

Emotional well-being Exploration:

Research in emotional wellness keeps on investigating the hereditary and natural variables adding to different mental problems. This exploration illuminates treatment approaches and mediations.

Public Arrangement and Instruction:

The discussion has suggestions for public approach, particularly in regions like training and medical services. Strategies might have to consider the association between hereditary inclinations and ecological impacts in resolving social issues.

Biotechnology and Moral Contemplations:

As biotechnology progresses, moral conversations around quality altering, hereditary upgrade, and the potential for unseen side-effects are continuous. Guaranteeing dependable and moral utilization of hereditary innovations stays a basic concern.

2.1 The Role of Genetics in Animal Behavior

Creature conduct is an interesting and complex field of study that tries to comprehend how and why creatures connect with their current circumstance, one another, and themselves. While ecological elements assume a critical part in shaping a creature's way of behaving, hereditary qualities likewise has a significant impact in deciding their natural inclinations and reactions. In this paper, we will investigate the job of hereditary qualities in creature conduct, analyzing how hereditary elements impact different parts of conduct, from basic impulses to complex social ways of behaving.

Hereditary qualities and Conduct: An Outline

Hereditary qualities alludes to the investigation of qualities and their job in deciding a person's physical and social attributes. Qualities are portions of DNA that code for explicit proteins or utilitarian components inside a creature.

They are acquired from a creature's folks, and varieties in qualities can prompt hereditary variety inside an animal varieties.

With regards to conduct, hereditary qualities assumes a vital part in two essential ways:

Inborn Way of behaving: These are ways of behaving that are hereditarily designed and don't need learning. Intrinsic ways of behaving are much of the time set off by unambiguous improvements or circumstances and are exceptionally saved inside an animal groups. Instances of intrinsic ways of behaving incorporate reflexes, mating customs, and movement designs.

Hereditary Inclination: While not all parts of a creature's way of behaving are designed, hereditary elements can make an inclination or helplessness to specific ways of behaving. These inclinations impact how a creature answers natural prompts and encounters.

Hereditary effects on creature conduct have been concentrated on broadly in different species, and exploration keeps on revealing insight into the multifaceted exchange among qualities and conduct.

Intrinsic Ways of behaving and Hereditary Determinism

Natural ways of behaving are among the most striking instances of hereditary determinism in creature conduct. These ways of behaving are encoded in a creature's DNA, and they manifest in unsurprising ways in light of explicit triggers. A few eminent instances of inborn ways of behaving and their hereditary premise include:

Reflexes: Straightforward reflexes, like the withdrawal of a hand from a hot item, are constrained by hereditary instruments that guarantee a quick and programmed reaction to a specific upgrade.

Instinctual Ways of behaving: In numerous species, ways of behaving like settling, scrounging, and hunter aversion are hereditarily customized. For instance, the web-building conduct of a bug still up in the air and requires no learning.

Mating Ceremonies: Romance and mating customs are frequently designed in creatures, with explicit ways of behaving and shows directed by hereditary qualities. In some bird species, for example, many-sided romance moves and melodies are hereditarily encoded and profoundly unambiguous.

Relocation: The capacity to move is one more illustration of intrinsic way of behaving. Numerous creatures, for example, birds, ocean turtles, and ruler butterflies, have a hereditary inclination to leave on significant distance excursions to track down food or reasonable favorable places.

Natural Hostility: Forceful ways of behaving in creatures, like regional guard, are in many cases impacted by hereditary variables that decide a singular's inclination to take part in fierce ways of behaving.

The hereditary reason for these inborn ways of behaving is irrefutable and has added to how we might interpret the transformative benefits presented by such ways of behaving. Inborn ways of behaving give an animal categories a set-up of procedures that improve their endurance and conceptive achievement.

Hereditary Inclination and Natural Impact

While numerous parts of creature conduct not entirely set in stone, it is critical to perceive that hereditary qualities doesn't work in confinement. Ecological factors likewise assume a basic part in shaping way of behaving, and as a rule, conduct results from a perplexing exchange between hereditary inclinations and natural impacts.

Learning and Experience: The statement of hereditary inclinations frequently relies upon learning and experience. For instance, a bird's hereditary inclination to construct a particular sort of home might be impacted by ecological factors, for example, the accessibility of settling materials and openness to other birds' homes.

Quality Climate Connections: Quality climate cooperations are vital in understanding how hereditary inclinations are communicated. Similar hereditary inclination in two people might prompt various ways of behaving assuming that they are presented to various ecological circumstances.

Epigenetics: Epigenetics is the investigation of heritable changes in quality articulation that don't include modifications to the fundamental DNA grouping. Epigenetic changes can be impacted by natural factors and can influence how qualities are communicated, prompting varieties in conduct.

Phenotypic Versatility: Numerous creatures display phenotypic pliancy, which is the capacity to change their way of behaving or actual attributes in light of ecological circumstances. This pliancy frequently permits creatures to adjust to changing conditions and improve their way of behaving.

Instances of Hereditary Inclination and Natural Impact

Hostility in Canines: Some canine varieties have hereditary inclinations for specific ways of behaving, for example, crowding, monitoring, or recovering. Be that as it may, the statement of these ways of behaving can be impacted via preparing, socialization, and natural elements. For instance, a canine with a hereditary inclination for hostility might show this conduct all the more noticeably whenever brought up in an oppressive or careless climate.

Maternal Consideration in Rodents: Female rodents ordinarily have a hereditary inclination for maternal ways of behaving. Be that as it may, the outflow of maternal consideration can be affected by factors like hormonal changes during pregnancy, the presence of the litter, and the nature of the settling site.

Tune Learning in Birds: Some bird species, for example, canaries and zebra finches, have a hereditary inclination for melody learning. Be that as it may, the quality and intricacy of the melody can be impacted by openness to other birds' tunes during a basic time of improvement.

Human Animosity: Human hostility is impacted by both hereditary inclination and ecological elements. Hereditary variables might add to a singular's vulnerability to forceful ways of behaving, however ecological impacts, like openness to savagery, relational intricacies, and social standards, additionally assume a huge part.

Hereditary Premise of Intricate Ways of behaving

Hereditary qualities likewise assumes a part in additional complicated ways of behaving that are not totally designed yet include a mix of hereditary inclination and natural impact. These ways of behaving include:

Perception: The capacity to learn, reason, and tackle issues is affected by hereditary elements. Varieties in qualities related with mental capabilities can affect a singular's capacity to learn and adjust.

Character: Character qualities, like extraversion, neuroticism, and pleasantness, have a hereditary premise. Nonetheless, character improvement is additionally impacted by life encounters and natural variables.

Habit-forming Ways of behaving: Hereditary elements can impact a singular's weakness to dependence. Certain qualities are related with an expanded gamble of substance misuse, however ecological elements, like openness to drugs, likewise assume a significant part.

Social Ways of behaving: The capacity to frame social bonds, understand others, and participate in friendly associations is impacted by hereditary qualities. Varieties in qualities connected with social way of behaving can influence a singular's interactive abilities and propensities.

Research there has recognized explicit qualities and hereditary varieties related with complex ways of behaving. Nonetheless, it is fundamental to underline that the statement of these hereditary inclinations is adjusted by natural elements, including early educational encounters, social impacts, and social collaborations.

Hereditary Strategies in the Investigation of Creature Conduct

Progresses in hereditary qualities and genomics have upset the investigation of creature conduct. Analysts presently utilize different hereditary strategies to examine the hereditary premise of conduct. A portion of these methods include:

Twin and Family Studies: In human and a few creature populaces, twin and family concentrates on contrast the ways of behaving of people and differing levels of hereditary relatedness. These investigations can assist with assessing the heritability of explicit ways of behaving.

Quantitative Hereditary qualities: Quantitative hereditary qualities investigates the hereditary premise of complicated characteristics, including conduct, by inspecting the level of hereditary variety inside a populace. It gives evaluations of heritability and the impact of hereditary qualities on attribute variety.

Up-and-comer Quality Examinations: Scientists recognize explicit qualities related with conduct and afterward research their job in creature conduct. These examinations frequently include contrasting the way of behaving of creatures and without explicit quality changes.

Extensive Affiliation Studies (GWAS): GWAS recognize hereditary varieties related with social characteristics by looking at the whole genome. This approach can uncover hereditary markers connected to explicit ways of behaving.

Epigenetics: Epigenetic studies analyze alterations to DNA and chromatin that influence quality articulation. Analysts examine how epigenetic changes impact conduct and whether they can be acquired or affected by ecological elements.

Atomic Science Strategies: Sub-atomic science procedures, for example, quality articulation examination and RNA sequencing, permit analysts to concentrate on quality movement comparable to conduct.

These hereditary methods have given important experiences into the hereditary premise of creature conduct, from straightforward impulses to complex mental cycles.

Commonsense Uses of Hereditary Exploration in Creature Conduct

Understanding the hereditary premise of creature conduct has commonsense applications in different fields, including:

Creature Preservation: Hereditary exploration can assist progressives recognize and safeguard populaces with explicit social transformations, for example, transient examples, that are basic for the endurance of an animal types.

Creature Government assistance: Information on the hereditary premise of conduct can illuminate creature government assistance works on, including the plan of hostage conditions and reproducing programs that record for a creature's social inclinations.

Agribusiness and Animals: Hereditary examination in animals can prompt the improvement of creature strains with wanted conduct characteristics, like accommodation or upgraded abilities to scavenge.

Neurobiology and Medication: Understanding the hereditary premise of conduct in creature models can give bits of knowledge into the hereditary underpinnings of human ways of behaving and psychological well-being conditions.

Organic and Developmental Exploration: Hereditary examination is central to figuring out the advancement of ways of behaving and variations across various species.

Challenges and Moral Contemplations

The investigation of the hereditary premise of creature conduct isn't without challenges and moral contemplations. A portion of these difficulties and contemplations include:

Intricacy of Conduct: Creature conduct is complex and impacted by a huge swath of qualities, ecological variables, and quality climate communications. Recognizing the particular qualities answerable for complex ways of behaving is testing.

Moral Treatment of Creatures: Exploration on the hereditary premise of creature conduct ought to focus on the moral treatment of creatures. Moral rules and creature government assistance guidelines should be continued in all examination including creatures.

Hereditary Determinism: The investigation of hereditary qualities in conduct should try not to advance hereditary determinism, which distorts the connection among qualities and conduct. Conduct is a result of both hereditary and ecological elements.

Protection and Assent: In human social hereditary qualities, issues connected with security and informed assent are of most extreme significance. Moral contemplations should direct the assortment and utilization of hereditary information connected with conduct.

Potential for Abuse: Hereditary data about conduct can be abused or misjudged, prompting trashing or prejudicial practices. Moral shields should be set up to forestall such abuse.

2.2 The Influence of Environmental Factors

The turn of events and conduct of living life forms are significantly impacted by natural elements. These variables include an extensive variety of physical, natural, and social components that encompass and interface with people all through their lives. The effect of ecological variables is critical, as they assume a crucial part in molding a creature's turn of events, ways of behaving, and generally prosperity. In this article, we will investigate the impact of ecological elements, featuring their consequences for various parts of human and creature life.

Early Life Climate and Improvement

The climate a singular experiences during early life, especially during the pre-birth and early post pregnancy stages, can meaningfully affect physical and mental turn of events. Factors like maternal sustenance, openness to poisons, and pre-birth pressure can influence the improvement of an unborn kid. Dietary lacks or openness to destructive substances during pregnancy can prompt birth deserts, formative deferrals, and medical conditions in kids.

The post pregnancy climate, including the nature of providing care, sustenance, and openness to youth schooling, likewise fundamentally influences mental and close to home turn of events. Youngsters brought up in supporting, animating conditions will generally foster better mental and interactive abilities. On the other hand, youngsters brought up in conditions lacking daily encouragement and scholarly excitement might confront formative difficulties and conduct issues.

Nourishment and Wellbeing

Nourishment is a major natural component that impacts human wellbeing and prosperity. A fair eating regimen with sufficient supplements is fundamental for actual development, mental turn of events, and in general wellbeing.

Lack of healthy sustenance during youth can prompt hindered development, mental shortages, and an expanded weakness to sicknesses.

Additionally, the accessibility of clean drinking water and admittance to legitimate sterilization essentially influence wellbeing. The absence of clean water can prompt waterborne sicknesses and unfortunate sterilization works on, adding to the spread of diseases.

Openness to Poisons and Contamination

Openness to ecological poisons and contaminations can inconveniently affect both human and creature wellbeing. Air contamination, water contamination, and openness to dangerous synthetics can bring about an extensive variety of medical conditions, including respiratory problems, cardiovascular illnesses, and formative issues in kids.

One prominent model is the effect of lead openness on mental advancement in youngsters. Lead harming, frequently brought about by openness to toxic paints or debased water, can prompt irreversible harm to the creating cerebrum, bringing about learning inabilities and conduct issues.

Social Climate and Emotional well-being

The social climate, including relational intricacies, peer cooperations, and cultural impacts, significantly affects emotional wellness and prosperity. Social help, a sustaining family climate, and positive friend connections can add to profound versatility and emotional wellness.

On the other hand, people presented to unfavorable social conditions, like maltreatment, disregard, or social segregation, are at a higher gamble of creating psychological well-being issues, including misery, tension, and post-horrendous pressure problem.

Instructive Open doors

Admittance to quality schooling is a huge ecological component that shapes a person's mental turn of events, abilities, and future open doors. Instructive open doors can differ broadly founded on geographic area, financial status, and social variables.

Excellent schooling gives people the information and abilities important to seek after an extensive variety of profession ways and add to cultural turn of events. Then again, restricted admittance to schooling can propagate social imbalances and frustrate individual and financial development.

Social and Cultural Standards

Social and cultural standards fundamentally impact human and creature conduct. These standards direct satisfactory ways of behaving, values, and customs inside a general public. People gain and incorporate these standards since early on, and they shape a singular's social associations and feeling of character.

Social standards can impact ways of behaving connected with marriage, family, orientation jobs, religion, and relational connections. They can likewise influence dietary decisions, clothing standards, and day to day schedules. Essentially, cultural standards, like legitimate and moral norms, guide a singular's moral and lawful obligations inside a local area.

Cataclysmic events and Environmental Change

Ecological variables can likewise incorporate cataclysmic events and environmental change. The event of catastrophic events, like quakes, tropical storms, or floods, can devastatingly affect human and creature populaces. These occasions can bring about the deficiency of lives, removal, and critical harm to foundation.

Environmental change, driven by human exercises and natural elements, presents long haul dangers to biological systems and human social orders. Increasing temperatures, outrageous climate occasions, and modified precipitation examples can affect agribusiness, water assets, and the spread of sicknesses. These progressions have wide arriving at ramifications for human and creature populaces.

Ecological Enhancement and Prosperity

Natural improvement is an idea applied in creature care and brain research to upgrade the prosperity of hostage creatures. It includes giving creatures animating conditions that empower regular ways of behaving and mental commitment. Advancement exercises can incorporate novel items, riddles, and open doors for social cooperation.

In zoos and protection focuses, ecological enhancement is essential for decreasing pressure, working on emotional wellness, and advancing the statement of normal ways of behaving in hostage creatures. The arrangement of advanced conditions is intended to impersonate the circumstances viewed as in the wild, giving mental feeling and actual activity.

Metropolitan and Provincial Conditions

Whether an individual lives in a metropolitan or country climate can essentially impact their way of life, valuable open doors, and prosperity. Metropolitan conditions will generally offer more admittance to medical care, schooling, and work open doors, however they can likewise bring more elevated levels of contamination and stress. Rustic conditions might give cleaner air and a calmer speed of life however can need admittance to fundamental administrations and open positions.

The decision of living climate can affect a singular's personal satisfaction and generally speaking wellbeing. It can likewise impact way of life decisions, for example, practice propensities, dietary inclinations, and admittance to sporting exercises.

2.3 Lorenz's Insights on Innate Behavior

Konrad Lorenz, an Austrian zoologist and one of the establishing figures of ethology, made critical commitments to how we might interpret natural conduct in creatures. His work stressed the job of hereditary qualities and natural ways of behaving in the animals of the world collectively. Lorenz's experiences lastingly affect the area of ethology and our more extensive comprehension of creature conduct.

Engraving and Basic Periods:

Lorenz's momentous examination on engraving in waterfowl, especially geese and ducks, gave fundamental experiences into natural way of behaving. Engraving is a peculiarity wherein youthful creatures quickly and irreversibly structure connections to the main moving item they see during a particular basic period in their initial turn of events.

Lorenz's investigations included presenting youthful waterfowl to himself or other moving items during their basic period. He found that the creatures engraved on the primary item they experienced and would consequently follow it, showing major areas of strength for a to it. Lorenz's work showed the presence of an organically customized system that impacts a creature's social and mating ways of behaving.

Fixed Activity Examples (FAPs):

Lorenz likewise presented the idea of fixed activity designs (FAPs), which are cliché, untaught ways of behaving set off by unambiguous improvements. FAPs are intrinsic and designed into a creature's sensory system, permitting them to answer explicit ecological prompts with profoundly unsurprising ways of behaving. These ways of behaving are much of the time connected with endurance and multiplication.

For instance, Lorenz noticed FAPs in birds' home structure conduct. When a bird experiences explicit boosts, for example, seeing home materials, it will take part in a fixed and profoundly organized grouping of activities to construct a home. FAPs guarantee that critical endurance and conceptive ways of behaving are done effectively.

Intrinsic Delivering Instruments (IRMs):

Lorenz proposed the idea of natural delivering instruments (IRMs) to make sense of how explicit sign boosts trigger fixed activity designs. IRMs are brain instruments that perceive and answer explicit sign upgrades, starting the fitting FAP.

These instruments are naturally foreordained and designed into a creature's sensory system. They guarantee that creatures answer fittingly to pertinent natural signals, like seeing a possible mate or a hunter.

Sign Improvements and Releasers:

Lorenz's work likewise accentuated the meaning of sign upgrades or releasers in setting off natural ways of behaving. Sign upgrades are explicit, frequently exceptionally visual, hear-able, or olfactory signs that immediate a specific conduct in creatures. For example, in romance ceremonies of some bird species, guys answer the particular viewable signals given by females, similar to their plumage or body shows.

Lorenz's bits of knowledge into sign boosts and releasers featured the job of profoundly unambiguous triggers in shaping creature conduct. This understanding has wide ramifications in the investigation of creature correspondence and social collaborations.

2.4 The Interplay of Nature and Nurture in Animal Ways

The deep rooted discussion of nature versus sustain additionally holds huge pertinence in the domain of creature conduct. Nature alludes to the hereditary and inborn elements that impact conduct, while support envelops the ecological and experiential variables that shape it. As a general rule, the way of behaving of creatures is the consequence of a powerful interchange between these two powers.

Nature in Creature Conduct:

Hereditary elements assume a crucial part in forming natural ways of behaving in creatures. These natural ways of behaving, otherwise called impulses, are designed and don't need learning. They are frequently basic for a creature's endurance and conceptive achievement. For instance, transitory examples in birds, home structure in rodents, and hunter evasion in different species are natural ways of behaving encoded in a creature's hereditary cosmetics.

These ways of behaving are dependent upon normal determination and have advanced over ages to upgrade a creature's possibilities of endurance. Nature, in this unique circumstance, sets the essential structure for a creature's social collection.

Support in Creature Conduct:

Natural factors, encounters, and advancing likewise apply a critical impact on creature conduct. Creatures answer their environmental factors, adjust to evolving conditions, and foster ways of behaving through openness and experience. Social cooperations with friends, guardians, and different individuals from similar species can prompt learning and the procurement of explicit ways of behaving.

For instance, the romance ceremonies of some bird species include complex moves and tunes, which are advanced by noticing conspecifics. This learned way of behaving is sustained through friendly communications and openness to the climate.

The Interchange:

The transaction among nature and support in creature conduct is a complicated and dynamic cycle. Qualities give the inclination or potential to specific ways of behaving, while the climate shapes the declaration of those ways of behaving.

Think about the case of hunter evasion in a types of little vertebrates. Hereditary inclinations might incorporate an uplifted aversion to the fragrance of hunters or the nature to freeze while detecting risk. In any case, the particular hunter scents that an individual figures out how to connect with risk and the viability of its freezing reaction rely upon its encounters and associations in the climate. This exchange among nature and support considers adaptability and transformation in conduct.

Also, ecological variables can impact the timing and articulation of hereditary inclinations. For example, the planning of transient conduct in birds can be impacted by natural signs like changing day length, temperature, and food accessibility. These outer elements can set off the hereditary inclination for relocation brilliantly.

Chapter 3

Animal Communication: The Language of the Wild

The animals of the world collectively is an immense and various domain, over-flowing with a large number of animal types, each with its own special approaches to conveying. From the musical tunes of birds to the multifaceted moves of honey bees, the universe of creature correspondence is an interesting and complex subject that has caught the creative mind of researchers, naturalists, and creature lovers for quite a long time. In this 2000-word investigation, we will dig into the complex and different ways creatures speak with each other, revealing insight into the uncommon language of nature.

Part 1: The Underpinnings of Creature Correspondence

Correspondence is a central part of life, permitting creatures to trade data and guarantee their endurance. In the set of all animals, correspondence takes on various structures, all determined by the need to pass essential messages on to different individuals from their species. This section will give an essential comprehension of the standards fundamental creature correspondence.

1.1. The Meaning of Correspondence

Creatures impart for different purposes, including tracking down mates, advance notice of risk, laying out strength, and organizing bunch exercises. Powerful correspondence is significant for their endurance and conceptive achievement.

1.2. Modalities of Creature Correspondence

Creatures utilize different correspondence modalities, including vocalizations, visual presentations, synthetic signs, and material prompts. Every methodology is custom-made to suit the species' biological specialty and social construction.

1.3. The Job of Signs and Prompts

Signals are deliberate activities or designs intended to pass on data, like bird melodies, while prompts are unexpected marks of a creature's presence or state, similar to impressions or fragrance marks. Both assume significant parts in correspondence.

Vocal Correspondence in the Collective of animals

Sound is one of the most pervasive types of correspondence in the collective of animals. This section investigates the universe of vocal correspondence and its importance in different species.

2.1. Birds: The Virtuosos of Melody

Birds are prestigious for their musical melodies, which serve different capabilities, including drawing in mates, a safeguarding area, and cautioning of hunters. We will dive into the complicated universe of avian vocalizations and how they adjust to various biological specialties.

2.2. Warm blooded animals: Thunders, Whistles, and Snaps

Warm blooded animals likewise use vocalizations to pass on data. From the profound thunders of lions to the frightful tunes of humpback whales, we will investigate the variety of mammalian vocal correspondence and its part in friendly associations.

2.3. Creatures of land and water: Night Songs

Frogs and amphibians utilize different calls to draw in mates and lay out region. Their exceptional vocalizations have developed to suit the acoustic conditions of their environments, bringing about an enamoring cluster of calls.

Visual Signals and Shows

Numerous creatures depend on visual signs to impart, frequently utilizing non-verbal communication, shading, and other obvious signals to pass data on to conspecifics and hunters. This part dives into the domain of visual correspondence in nature.

3.1. Romance Showcases

Romance showcases are complex ceremonies utilized by creatures to draw in mates. Models incorporate the peacock's gaudy tail feathers, the unpredictable moves of cranes, and the intricate presentations of bowerbirds.

3.2. Cautioning Presentations

Visual signs can likewise be utilized to dissuade hunters or contenders. This incorporates the bright admonition examples of toxic frogs, the danger presentations of reptiles, and the admonition shades of stinging bugs.

3.3. Social Ordered progression and Predominance

In numerous species, visual presentations assume a significant part in laying out friendly pecking orders. Creatures use stances, motions, and other viewable prompts to convey their status inside the gathering. Models remember the extremely confident man's predominant position for a wolf pack and the posing of meerkats in sentinel obligation.

Synthetic Correspondence

Compound signs assume an essential part in creature correspondence, permitting living beings to pass data on through fragrance and pheromones. In this section, we investigate what substance correspondence means for conduct in the animals of the world collectively.

4.1. Pheromones: The Language of Fragrances

Pheromones are substance flags that send data about a creature's conceptive status, regional limits, and other significant messages. We will examine the assorted manners by which creatures use pheromones to convey, from checking an area to drawing in mates.

4.2. Insects and Termites: Compound Realms

Social bugs, like insects and termites, depend intensely on substance correspondence to organize their perplexing social orders. They use pheromones to pass on messages about food sources, dangers, and settlement association.

4.3. The Astonishing Feeling of Smell

A few creatures have an unquestionably intense feeling of smell, permitting them to recognize and decipher synthetic signs with surprising accuracy. We will analyze the olfactory capacities of different species and their job in correspondence.

Material and Sensation Correspondence

Material and sensation correspondence is frequently ignored however is similarly as fundamental in the animals of the world collectively. This part investigates the manners in which creatures utilize actual touch and body developments to convey.

5.1. Social Holding and Preparing

Actual contact is vital for social holding in numerous species. Primates groom each other to fortify social ties, while elephants utilize material communications to convey consolation and backing.

5.2. Fun loving Developments

Youthful creatures frequently take part in perky developments as a type of correspondence and social turn of events. Play battling, pursuing, and different exercises are fundamental for creating vital abilities and social associations.

5.3. Regional Presentations

A few creatures use body developments and actual stances to guard their regions. This incorporates the head-swaying of anoles, the push-ups of reptiles, and the intricate moves of bumble bees while protecting their hive.

Complex Correspondence Frameworks

In a few creature animal groups, correspondence is strikingly complex, including the mix of different modalities and the utilization of conceptual ideas. This section investigates the complex correspondence frameworks tracked down in different animals.

6.1. Dolphins and Whales: The Language of the Oceans

Cetaceans, like dolphins and whales, are known for their perplexing correspondence frameworks. They utilize a blend of snaps, whistles, and body developments to pass on an extensive variety of data and keep up with many-sided social designs.

6.2. Bumble bees: The Dance of Headings

Bumble bees utilize a dance language to impart the area of food sources to their nestmates. The waggle dance, for example, passes both distance and heading on to direct different honey bees to nectar-rich blossoms.

6.3. Primates: The Intricacy of Signals and Vocalizations

Primates, including chimpanzees and bonobos, have rich correspondence frameworks that consolidate the two vocalizations and motions. They utilize these signs to lay out friendly bonds, share data about food sources, and direction bunch exercises.

The Advancement of Creature Correspondence

The variety of correspondence methodologies in the set of all animals brings up captivating issues about the developmental beginnings and variations of these frameworks. This part dives into the advancement of creature correspondence.

7.1. Coevolution of Signs and Collectors

Correspondence frameworks frequently develop couple with the tactile and mental capacities of the beneficiary. Species that share similar climate and natural specialties might foster remarkable correspondence frameworks to limit obstruction.

7.2. The Effect of Social Construction

The social construction of an animal groups can fundamentally impact the development of its correspondence frameworks. Single creatures might depend on visual and compound signals, while social creatures frequently foster complex vocal and gestural dialects.

7.3. The Job of Learning

Numerous creatures, particularly primates and cetaceans, display learning and social transmission of correspondence signals. This takes into account the improvement of provincial vernaculars and the transformation of correspondence to evolving conditions.

Human-Creature Correspondence

The limits of creature correspondence reach out to our cooperations with creatures, trained and wild. This part investigates the manners by which people speak with and grasp creatures.

8.1. Tamed Creatures: Correspondence and Friendship

People have created different types of correspondence with tamed creatures, like canines, ponies, and felines. These bonds are based on trust, understanding, and shared encounters.

8.2. Ethology and Field Exploration

Ethologists and handle analysts have made critical commitments to how we might interpret creature correspondence. By noticing and deciphering the way of behaving of wild creatures, we gain bits of knowledge into their complex correspondence frameworks.

8.3. Preservation and Ecotourism

Successful correspondence with wild creatures is urgent for protection endeavors and ecotourism. Eco-guides and progressives utilize a scope of systems to convey the significance of safeguarding normal territories and regarding untamed life.

3.1 Vocalizations and Body Language

Vocalizations and non-verbal communication are general types of correspondence that rise above language obstructions. While people depend intensely on verbal correspondence, the collective of animals uses vocalizations and non-verbal communication to pass on fundamental data. These non-verbal types of articulation are central to grasping the ways of behaving, feelings, and collaborations of the two people and creatures. we will dive into the meaning of vocalizations and non-verbal communication, revealing insight into their widespread job in correspondence.

Vocalizations in the Animals of the world collectively

1.1. The Variety of Creature Sounds

The collective of animals is packed with different and extraordinary vocalizations. From the tunes of birds to the thunders of lions, various species have advanced explicit sounds custom fitted to their natural specialties and social designs.

1.2. Correspondence Capabilities

Creature vocalizations serve a heap of capabilities, including drawing in mates, advance notice of risk, a stamping area, and organizing bunch exercises. Understanding these capabilities is urgent to deciphering creature conduct.

1.3. Variations to Acoustic Conditions

Creatures have adjusted their vocalizations to suit the acoustic properties of their surroundings. For example, marine warm blooded creatures have developed to impart submerged, where sound voyages uniquely in contrast to in the air.

The Expressive Force of Human Vocalizations

2.1. Language and Feeling

People convey through words as well as through the tone, pitch, and mood of their voices. These vocal components convey feelings, goals, and mentalities, giving essential setting to communicated in language.

2.2. Non-Verbal Vocal Signs

Beyond anything that can be put into words and tone, people utilize non-verbal vocal prompts like giggling, moans, and vocal fillers (e.g., "um" and "uh") to communicate sentiments and responses. These prompts assume a critical part in conveying meaning.

2.3. Multifaceted Contrasts

While a few vocal articulations are all inclusive, others fluctuate across societies. Understanding the social setting of vocalizations is fundamental for compelling correspondence in a globalized world.

Non-verbal communication in the Animals of the world collectively

3.1. Stances and Motions

Non-verbal communication in the animals of the world collectively is passed on through stances, motions, and developments. Creatures utilize these non-verbal prompts to lay out predominance, convey accommodation, or sign hostility.

3.2. Romance Customs

Romance in the creature world frequently includes complex non-verbal communication, like the moves of birds of heaven or the showcases of bowerbirds. These ceremonies are basic for drawing in mates.

3.3. Social Progressive systems

Social creatures depend on non-verbal communication to lay out and keep up with progressive systems inside their gatherings. Strength shows, compliant stances, and affiliative ways of behaving all assume a part in friendly connections.

The Expressive Force of Human Non-verbal communication

4.1. Looks

The human face is a rich material for non-verbal demeanor. Looks convey many feelings, from euphoria and trouble to outrage and astound. Understanding these signs is fundamental for deciphering social communications.

4.2. Stance and Development

Human non-verbal communication stretches out past the face, incorporating stance and development. Folding one's arms might flag protectiveness, while open and loosened up stances show solace and agreeability.

4.3. Microexpressions

Microexpressions are transient, compulsory looks that uncover covered feelings. Perceiving and deciphering these microexpressions can give further bits of knowledge into human way of behaving.

The Development of Vocalizations and Non-verbal communication

5.1. Transformative Beginnings

Vocalizations and non-verbal communication have profound transformative roots. They have created as versatile systems for correspondence, assisting organic entities with exploring their surroundings and social designs.

5.2. Cross-Species Correlations

Concentrating on vocalizations and non-verbal communication across species permits us to recognize shared transformative standards. For instance, similitudes in strength shows among primates and people propose normal family line.

5.3. Variations to Human Culture

The advancement of human vocalizations and non-verbal communication has been affected by the improvement of intricate social orders. As people adjusted to bunch living, their correspondence frameworks turned out to be more perplexing and nuanced.

The Force of Deciphering Non-Verbal Signals

6.1. Compassion and Association

The capacity to peruse and decipher vocalizations and non-verbal communication is essential for building compassion and shaping significant associations with others. Perceiving feelings and aims improves relational connections.

6.2. Compromise

Understanding non-verbal signs can assist with settling clashes and false impressions. By perceiving indications of stress or uneasiness, people can change their correspondence to advance collaboration and congruity.

6.3. Non-Verbal Correspondence in the Computerized Age

In an undeniably computerized world, non-verbal signs are much of the time lost or misjudged. Understanding the constraints and likely traps of virtual correspondence is fundamental for successful internet based associations.

3.2 Signals, Cues, and Messages

Correspondence is an essential part of life, permitting living beings to pass on data and guarantee their endurance. In the many-sided universe of correspondence, signals, prompts, and messages assume vital parts. These components act as the structure blocks of correspondence, working with cooperations and trades of data across the collective of animals. In this 1400-word investigation, we will dig into the meaning of signs, prompts, and messages, revealing insight into the unpretentious language that underlies correspondence in the two people and the normal world.

The Groundworks of Correspondence

1.1. The Need of Correspondence

Correspondence is a crucial instrument for endurance and conceptive accomplishment across species. It empowers living beings to trade data about food sources, hunters, mates, and other fundamental parts of life.

1.2. The Job of Signs

Signals are purposeful activities or designs used to pass on data. They can be visual, hear-able, olfactory, or material and are in many cases a result of regular determination, finely tuned to fill a particular need.

1.3. The Accidental Prompts

As opposed to signals, prompts are accidental marks of a life form's presence, state, or conduct. These prompts can be gotten by others and may not be guaranteed to fill the singular's essential need yet can in any case pass on significant data.

Visual Signs

2.1. Shading and Examples

Numerous creatures use tinge and examples on their bodies as visual signs. These signs can convey data about their wellbeing, age, and availability to mate. Models incorporate the dynamic plumage of male birds and the admonition shades of harmful creatures.

2.2. Conduct Showcases

Visual signals frequently manifest as social presentations. Romance moves, regional stances, and danger shows are utilized by creatures to pass their goals and inspirations on to other people.

2.3. Cover

A few creatures utilize visual signs to mix into their environmental elements, successfully becoming imperceptible to hunters or prey. The chameleon's capacity to change its skin tone and example is a great representation of this system.

Hear-able Signs

3.1. Birdsong

Birds are famous for their melodic tunes, which serve numerous capabilities, including drawing in mates, a safeguarding area, and cautioning of hunters. These hear-able signs are exceptional to every species and can convey data about a person's hereditary wellness.

3.2. Mammalian Vocalizations

Well evolved creatures likewise depend on vocalizations to impart. Thunders, snarls, and cries are frequently used to lay out strength, ready gathering individuals to risk, or direction bunch exercises. For example, wolves utilize yelling to keep up with bunch union.

3.3. Land and water proficient Calls

Creatures of land and water use vocalizations, like croaks and twitters, to convey in various settings. Frog calls are fundamental for drawing in mates and laying an out area, and they can be exceptionally species-explicit.

Olfactory and Synthetic Signs

4.1. Pheromones: Substance Couriers

Pheromones are synthetic signals that communicate data about a creature's conceptive status, regional limits, and other pivotal messages. These scent signs assume a critical part in creature correspondence.

4.2. Checking Region

Numerous creatures, from large felines to little vertebrates, use fragrance stamping to characterize their domains. These compound signs pass on data about a singular's presence and strength inside a given region.

4.3. Social Holding

Synthetic signs can likewise work with social holding, as found in the preparing conduct of primates and the exchange of fragrance prompts during actual contact. These signs assist with fortifying gathering union and connections.

Material Signs

5.1. Social Preparing

Material correspondence is many times communicated through friendly prepping. Primates, specifically, use preparing to lay out and support social bonds inside their gatherings. Preparing gives both physical and close to home solace.

5.2. Lively Collaborations

Youthful creatures participate in energetic connections as a type of material correspondence. Play battling, wrestling, and different exercises assist them with creating pivotal physical and interactive abilities.

5.3. Mating Customs

Material prompts are likewise noticeable in mating customs. For example, male insects utilize complex romance moves to pass their expectations and convince females on to mate.

The Intricacy of Human Correspondence

6.1. Verbal and Non-Verbal Signs

Human correspondence includes both verbal and non-verbal signs. Verbal language passes on unequivocal data, while non-verbal signals, like non-verbal communication, looks, and manner of speaking, impart feelings, purpose, and setting.

6.2. Emojis and Emoticon

In the computerized age, emojis and emoticon act as compact visual signs to convey feelings and responses in composed correspondence, overcoming any barrier between text-based and up close and personal cooperations.

6.3. Social Varieties

Social standards can altogether impact the translation of signs, prompts, and messages. Signals, articulations, and manners can differ broadly between societies, prompting likely miscommunications in multifaceted associations.

Transformative Importance

7.1. Coevolution of Signs and Beneficiaries

Correspondence frameworks frequently coevolve with the tactile and mental capacities of the beneficiary. Over the long haul, species that share a similar climate might foster extraordinary correspondence frameworks to limit obstruction.

7.2. The Job of Learning

Numerous creatures, particularly friendly species, show learning and social transmission of correspondence signals. This takes into consideration the advancement of local vernaculars and the transformation of correspondence to evolving conditions.

7.3. Versatile Benefit

The capacity to utilize and decipher signals, prompts, and messages is a versatile benefit that has advanced in different species. Compelling correspondence upgrades an organic entity's capacity to make due, duplicate, and explore its current circumstance.

The Force of Deciphering and Confusing Signs

8.1. The Expertise of Translation

The capacity to decipher signals, prompts, and messages is a principal expertise in the animals of the world collectively and for people. It empowers people to go with informed choices, structure social bonds, and explore complex social scenes.

8.2. Confusion and Miscommunication

Confusion of signals can prompt misconstruing, struggle, and botched open doors in both human and creature cooperations. Perceiving the potential for miscommunication is the most important phase in further developing correspondence.

8.3. Sympathy and Association

Grasping the nuances of signs, signals, and messages can encourage compassion and association. Perceiving the feelings, necessities, and expectations of others considers more significant and amicable connections.

3.3 Lorenz's Observations on Animal Communication

Konrad Lorenz, an Austrian zoologist, and ethologist, made critical commitments to the investigation of creature conduct, especially in the space of creature correspondence. Lorenz's spearheading work shed light on how creatures speak with one another, and his perceptions significantly affect the area of ethology, how we might interpret advancement, and the connections among people and the normal world. we will dive into Lorenz's perceptions on creature correspondence, giving experiences into his earth shattering examination and its persevering through pertinence.

The Groundworks of Ethology

1.1. Ethology: The Investigation of Creature Conduct

Ethology is the logical investigation of creature conduct in normal circumstances. Lorenz was an unmistakable figure in the improvement of ethology, which looks to grasp the development of conduct, the versatile worth of ways of behaving, and the job of correspondence in creature social orders.

1.2. Lorenz's Ethological Approach

Lorenz had faith in the significance of concentrating on creatures in their normal living spaces, noticing their ways of behaving and cooperations to acquire experiences into their social designs and correspondence frameworks. He was a defender of "Konrad Lorenz's engraved geese" as a great representation of ethological research.

1.3. Commitments to the Field

Lorenz's commitments to ethology reached out past creature correspondence. He mentioned significant objective facts on engraving, fixed activity designs, and ethograms, establishing the groundwork for the advanced investigation of creature conduct.

Engraving and Connection

2.1. Engraving as a Correspondence Interaction

Lorenz is popular for his work on engraving, a type of fast picking up during a delicate period in a creature's turn of events. Engraving assumes a basic part in parent-posterity correspondence and connection.

2.2. Lorenz's Test with Greylag Geese

Lorenz led an examination in which he raised a gathering of greylag geese from birth, engraving on himself as their guardian. This examination showed how engraving lays out major areas of strength for an among creatures and their guardians and assumes a vital part in parent-posterity correspondence.

2.3. Cross-Species Engraving

Lorenz's work additionally uncovered that engraving could happen across species. His perception of goslings engraving on him, a human, featured the pliancy of the engraving system and its significance in correspondence between various species.

Correspondence in Greylag Geese

3.1. Vocalizations and Stances

Lorenz noticed the complicated correspondence arrangement of greylag geese. They utilize a mix of vocalizations and stances to pass messages on to each other, going from keeping up with social bonds to cautioning each other to risk.

3.2. The "Upstanding Danger" Show

Lorenz recognized an unmistakable stance known as the "upstanding danger" show. Greylag geese utilize this stance to affirm strength and sign animosity. It fills in as a visual correspondence signal inside the social ordered progression of the gathering.

3.3. Relevant Correspondence

Lorenz underscored that the understanding of signs and signals ought to consider the setting where they happen. Greylag geese show various ways of behaving and vocalizations relying upon whether they are participating in romance, settling, or protecting their domain.

Lorenz's Impact on Human-Creature Connections

4.1. Experiences into Human Connection

Lorenz's perceptions on engraving and connection in creatures have offered experiences into human way of behaving. The connection hypothesis he created significantly affects the areas of brain science and childcare, featuring the significance of early connections in human turn of events.

4.2. Moral Contemplations

Lorenz's work with engraving additionally brought up moral issues about the effect of engraving on creature conduct and government assistance, particularly when creatures engraved on people. This conversation stays pertinent with regards to natural life protection and hostage creature care.

4.3. Protection and Ethology

Lorenz's work has added to how we might interpret creature conduct and correspondence, which is fundamental for protection endeavors. Ethological experiences assist researchers and preservationists with creating techniques to safeguard and oversee species in their common habitats.

Difficulties and Debates

5.1. Investigates of Lorenz's Techniques

Lorenz's accentuation on naturalistic perception, while important, has confronted analysis for the restricted command over factors and the potential for humanoid attribution in deciphering creature conduct.

5.2. Moral Worries

The moral contemplations of working with creatures, especially when they engrave on people, have ignited banter in mainstream researchers. Inquiries concerning creature government assistance and the effect of such connections on the creatures have been raised.

5.3. The Fate of Ethology

Ethology keeps on developing, integrating present day research procedures, including cutting edge innovations and quantitative strategies. Ethologists today endeavor to adjust the significance of naturalistic perception with the requirement for meticulousness in logical examination.

Heritage and Proceeding with Importance

6.1. Lorenz's Persevering through Heritage

Konrad Lorenz's work remains profoundly compelling in the areas of ethology, creature conduct, and brain research. His perceptions on creature correspondence and engraving have made an enduring imprint on how we might interpret the regular world.

6.2. Future Headings in Ethology

Ethologists and analysts keep on expanding upon Lorenz's work, using contemporary techniques to dive further into the complexities of creature correspondence, conduct, and perception. Understanding the language of creatures is critical to preservation, creature government assistance, and our relationship with the normal world.

6.3. Ethological Experiences for the Cutting edge World

Lorenz's perceptions help us to remember the significance of sympathy, empathy, and regard for creatures. In a world confronting environmental difficulties, ethological bits of knowledge offer important direction for how we collaborate with and safeguard the animals of the world collectively.

3.4 The Significance of Language in Animal Societies

Language is a noteworthy and exceptionally human characteristic, permitting us to pass on complex considerations, feelings, and data. While people have fostered a perplexing arrangement of communicated in and composed language, the collective of animals additionally depends on different types of correspondence to flourish inside their social orders. In this 1200-word investigation, we will dig into the meaning of language in creature social orders, uncovering how various species utilize their own correspondence frameworks to pass on urgent data and keep up with social attachment.

Characterizing Language in Creature Social orders

1.1. Correspondence as Language

Language, with regards to creature social orders, incorporates a great many signals, prompts, and messages utilized by creatures to pass on data. While these frameworks vary from human language, they are many-sided and profoundly adjusted to the requirements of every species.

1.2. Components of Creature Language

Creature language includes different components, including vocalizations, non-verbal communication, synthetic signs, and visual presentations. These components serve explicit capabilities inside every species' social construction and natural specialty.

1.3. Non-Phonetic Correspondence

While creature correspondence misses the mark on intricacy of human language, it is in any case profoundly viable in passing on data about mating, order, an area, and food sources. These non-semantic frameworks satisfy fundamental jobs inside creature social orders.

Vocal Correspondence

2.1. Birds: Experts of Melodic Language

Birds are eminent for their assorted and melodic tunes, which assume imperative parts in their social orders. These vocalizations are utilized for mating, regional guard, and social coordination, epitomizing the wealth of avian language.

2.2. Vertebrates: Thunders, Whistles, and Snaps

Warm blooded creatures additionally utilize vocal correspondence, with different species utilizing thunders, whistles, and snaps to pass on data. Lions' thunders state predominance and protect an area, while dolphins' snaps work with echolocation and gathering coordination.

2.3. Creatures of land and water: Brings in the Evening

Frogs and amphibians use vocalizations to draw in mates and lay out region. Their calls are the two species-explicit and custom fitted to their natural surroundings, exhibiting their transformation to their surroundings.

Visual Language and Body Stances

3.1. Romance Presentations

Visual language is many times utilized during romance ceremonies. Peacocks fan their lively tail plumes to draw in mates, while cranes take part in multifaceted moves to show their wellness and responsibility.

3.2. Social Order

Non-verbal communication and viewable prompts assume vital parts in laying out and keeping up with social orders inside creature social orders. Predominant people frequently show certain stances, while compliant individuals might show respectful ways of behaving.

3.3. Cautioning Showcases

Creatures likewise utilize visual signs to convey admonitions. For example, the strong admonition shades of specific bugs, for example, ladybugs and ruler butterflies, act as a visual obstacle to possible hunters.

Compound Signs and Olfactory Language

4.1. Pheromones: The Quiet Communicators

Pheromones are substance flags that pass on an extensive variety of data in creature social orders. They are especially significant for checking an area, demonstrating conceptive preparation, and organizing bunch exercises.

4.2. Insects and Termites: Compound Paths

Social bugs, including insects and termites, utilize compound signs to convey inside their states. Synthetic paths permit these bugs to share data about food sources, mark an area, and direction undertakings.

4.3. Aroma Checking in Warm blooded animals

Vertebrates, like large felines and canids, additionally depend on fragrance checking to convey inside their social orders. Fragrance markings lay out domain, demonstrate regenerative status, and convey individual personality.

The Job of Language in Friendly Union

5.1. Family and Overall vibes

Language in creature social orders is instrumental in keeping up with social attachment. It assists people with perceiving their family, cultivates collaboration, and advances bunch soundness.

5.2. Regenerative Achievement

Viable language assumes a significant part in creature multiplication. Romance customs and mating calls are fundamental for drawing in appropriate mates, guaranteeing hereditary variety, and adding to the endurance of posterity.

5.3. Asset Sharing and Coordination

Language permits creatures to convey about fundamental assets like food and water. It helps coordinate gathering exercises, for example, hunting in wolf packs or rummaging in friendly bug settlements.

Developmental Meaning of Creature Language

6.1. Developmental Transformations

The advancement of language in creature social orders addresses a versatile reaction to natural specialties, social designs, and the difficulties of endurance. These transformations empower species to convey successfully inside their surroundings.

6.2. Coevolution of Signs and Recipients

Language in creature social orders frequently coevolves with the tactile and mental capacities of the collectors. Over the long run, species that share a similar climate might foster remarkable correspondence frameworks to limit obstruction.

6.3. Impact on Human Language

The investigation of creature language has affected how we might interpret human language advancement. Perceiving shared traits and contrasts among creature and human correspondence reveals insight into the beginnings and advancement of language.

Human-Creature Connections

7.1. Tamed Creatures: The Language of Friendship

People have produced profound associations with trained creatures, from canines to ponies. These securities are based on common comprehension and correspondence, featuring the flexibility of creature language in human settings.

7.2. Ethology and Preservation

Ethologists and traditionalists depend on how they might interpret creature language to safeguard and oversee natural life. By unraveling creature correspondence frameworks, they can foster systems for protection and the safeguarding of normal territories.

7.3. Moral Contemplations

The investigation of creature language additionally raises moral worries, especially with regards to hostage creatures and untamed life the travel industry. Moral contemplations incorporate regarding creatures' normal correspondence designs and limiting interruption to their social orders.

Chapter 4

Territorial Behavior: Claiming, Defending, and Sharing

Regional way of behaving is an unavoidable and fundamental part of the animals of the world collectively, impacting how creatures cooperate with their surroundings, conspecifics (individuals from similar species), and different species. Whether it includes guaranteeing a fix of land for settling, protecting an asset rich region, or arranging the common utilization of a typical space, regional conduct assumes a crucial part in biology and creature endurance. In this complete 2000-word investigation, we will dive into the complexities of regional way of behaving, revealing insight into the systems, capabilities, and ramifications of asserting, shielding, and sharing domains in the normal world.

Characterizing Regional Way of behaving

1.1. Territoriality as a Crucial Idea

Regional way of behaving is a boundless peculiarity in the animals of the world collectively, happening in different species across different conditions. It includes the foundation, protection, and some of the time sharing of a particular region or asset, and it is driven by a scope of versatile capabilities.

1.2. Regional Reaches

Regional reaches can change generally in size and extension. From a little settling site guaranteed by a couple of birds to the sweeping domains of hunters like huge felines, the components of regions are impacted by natural variables and the species' science.

1.3. Territoriality Past the Set of all animals

Regional way of behaving isn't selective to the set of all animals. Plants, including trees and bushes, additionally participate in regional communications through contest for space, light, and supplements.

Elements of Regional Way of behaving

2.1. Asset Procurement and Usage

One essential capability of territoriality is to tie down admittance to fundamental assets, like food, water, and haven. By guaranteeing and safeguarding a region, people can guarantee a reliable inventory of these assets.

2.2. Propagation and Settling Destinations

Numerous species, especially birds and warm blooded creatures, lay out domains for conceptive purposes. Regional way of behaving permits people to get appropriate settling destinations and safeguard them from expected dangers.

2.3. Protection Against Contenders

Regional conduct effectively dissuades likely contenders. By guaranteeing and safeguarding domains, creatures decrease the probability of interruptions that could upset their day to day exercises or regenerative achievement.

Systems of Regional Way of behaving

3.1. Flagging and Correspondence

Regional creatures frequently use signs to lay out their presence and declare their responsibility for domain. These signs can incorporate vocalizations, visual showcases, and substance markings.

3.2. Forceful Connections

Actual hostility is a typical instrument for laying out and protecting domains. Creatures might participate in battles or shows to lay out predominance and figure out who controls the region.

3.3. Limit Support

Numerous regional creatures keep up with clear limits to delineate the restrictions of their domain. These limits might be set apart by actual elements, like aroma markings or visual milestones, to dissuade gatecrashers.

Kinds of Domains

4.1. Reproducing Regions

Rearing domains are laid out with the end goal of multiplication. Birds, for instance, frequently guarantee settling domains to draw in mates, lay eggs, and back their posterity.

4.2. Taking care of Regions

A few creatures lay out regions zeroed in on tying down admittance to food assets. For example, hummingbirds guard taking care of domains with plentiful nectar sources.

4.3. Home Reaches

Home reaches are more extensive than regions, incorporating the regions where creatures complete their day to day exercises. They might incorporate various rearing and taking care of regions inside the general reach.

Regional Conduct in Birds

5.1. Larks: Protecting Reproducing Domains

Larks are known for their vocal regional presentations, which are utilized to draw in mates and stop rivals. They lay out reproducing domains for settling and raising their young.

5.2. Raptors: Ruling the Skies

Flying predators, like birds and falcons, are regional in their hunting grounds. These regional reaches guarantee a steady inventory of prey to help their savage ways of life.

5.3. Waterfowl: Regions on the Water

Numerous waterfowl species, including ducks and swans, guarantee sea-going domains for settling and raising their posterity. These regions are normally situated on lakes, lakes, or waterways.

Regional Conduct in Warm blooded animals

6.1. Huge Felines: Predominant Hunters

Huge felines like lions and tigers are known for their regional way of behaving, which includes the guard of broad hunting domains. These domains assist with guaranteeing a steady food supply.

6.2. Canids: Shielding Social Designs

Wolves, foxes, and different canids lay out regions that help their social designs. Domains help in keeping up with bunch union and give admittance to assets to the pack.

6.3. Rodents: Tunnels and Regions

Numerous rat species, including ground squirrels and grassland canines, dig tunnels that act as both haven and region. They take part in regional questions to safeguard their tunnels and the assets around them.

Regional Conduct in Oceanic Conditions

7.1. Marine Warm blooded animals: Sea Domains

Marine warm blooded animals, like dolphins and seals, lay out domains in the huge region of the sea. These domains are frequently attached to explicit searching regions and assume a pivotal part in their endurance.

7.2. Coral Reefs: Submerged Land

Fish species occupying coral reefs lay out domains for safe house, multiplication, and admittance to food. Their bright shows and actual showdowns assist with characterizing these submerged spaces.

7.3. Freshwater Conditions: Stream and Waterway Regions

Freshwater fish, similar to salmon and trout, guarantee regions inside waterways and streams for generating and taking care of. These regions are in many cases focal points for rivalry and mating.

Sharing Domains and Covering Reaches

8.1. Covering Domains

Now and again, creatures might share covering domains, especially when assets are bountiful. Agreeable or regional resilience conduct can diminish the requirement for struggle.

8.2. Interspecific Regional Sharing

Various species may likewise share regions when their biological specialties and asset prerequisites don't essentially cover. These interspecific regional connections are driven by asset parceling.

8.3. Regional Questions

Clashes can emerge when two regional creatures experience each other inside covering ranges. These questions might prompt forceful showdowns or changes an in area limits.

Regional Way of behaving and Protection

9.1. Environment Protection

Understanding regional way of behaving is fundamental for preservation endeavors. Safeguarding basic living spaces guarantees the endurance of regional species by protecting their rearing, taking care of, and shielding regions.

9.2. Natural life The board

Preservationists and natural life supervisors use information on regional way of behaving to foster methodologies for saving undermined and jeopardized species. These endeavors might incorporate making safeguarded regions, overseeing human-natural life clashes, and reestablishing environment.

9.3. Moral Contemplations

Preservation endeavors should consider the moral ramifications of upsetting regional creatures or imparting spaces to them. Adjusting human and natural life interests is pivotal for fruitful conjunction.

4.1 Understanding Animal Territories

Regional way of behaving is a pervasive peculiarity in the collective of animals, enveloping different species across different biological systems. Creature regions are regions that people or gatherings guarantee, shield, and use for explicit purposes, like taking care of, rearing, or asylum. The idea of regions assumes a principal part in creature nature, conduct, and endurance. In this 1500-word investigation, we will dive into the multifaceted universe of creature regions, looking at the components, capabilities, and ramifications of these spatial cases in the regular world.

Characterizing Creature Domains

1.1. Regional Way of behaving: A Crucial Idea

Regional way of behaving is an inescapable and fundamental part of creature life, including the foundation, safeguard, and usage of explicit regions. Regions serve different biological and social capabilities, and their attributes can change generally among species.

1.2. Qualities of Domains

Creature regions might envelop a scope of elements, including actual space, assets, and, surprisingly, social connections. These qualities are impacted by species-explicit prerequisites and natural variables.

1.3. The Developmental Viewpoint

The advancement of regional way of behaving is profoundly attached to environmental variations. Over the long run, species have created systems to augment their wellness by effectively getting fundamental assets inside their domains.

Elements of Creature Regions

2.1. Asset Securing and Usage

One of the essential elements of creature domains is asset securing and usage. Domains assist people with tying down admittance to basic assets, like food, water, and haven.

2.2. Proliferation and Settling

Numerous creatures lay out regions for conceptive purposes. Reproducing domains give a protected and controlled climate for romance, mating, and the raising of posterity.

2.3. Safeguard Against Contenders

Regional conduct effectively prevents likely contenders from taking advantage of assets inside the guaranteed region. It decreases the gamble of interruptions and asset consumption, in this way helping the regional individual or gathering.

Systems of Regional Way of behaving

3.1. Flagging and Correspondence

Correspondence is a vital system for laying out and keeping up with regions. Creatures utilize different types of correspondence, including vocalizations, aroma markings, visual shows, and non-verbal communication, to convey possession and strength.

3.2. Forceful Collaborations

Forceful collaborations can assume a focal part in regional way of behaving, especially when limits are challenged. Actual showdowns or showcases of hostility might decide regional possession and progressive system.

3.3. Limit Upkeep

Keeping up with clear regional limits is significant for characterizing the degree of a domain. These limits can be set apart through visual tourist spots, fragrance markings, or other actual elements.

Kinds of Creature Regions

4.1. Reproducing Regions

Rearing domains are laid out with the end goal of proliferation. These domains give a controlled climate to romance, settling, and raising posterity, guaranteeing a higher opportunity of regenerative achievement.

4.2. Taking care of Domains

A few creatures lay out taking care of domains to tie down admittance to food assets. These regions are frequently connected with a dependable wellspring of nourishment, and guarding them guarantees the creature's endurance.

4.3. Home Reaches

Home reaches are more extensive than regions and incorporate the regions where creatures do their day to day exercises. They might incorporate various reproducing and taking care of domains, as well as extra asset regions.

Regional Conduct in Birds

5.1. Warblers: Vocal and Visual Showcases

Larks are known for their regional vocalizations and visual presentations. These ways of behaving are fundamental for drawing in mates, laying out rearing domains, and hindering adversaries.

5.2. Raptors: Guarding Hunting Regions

Flying predators, for example, falcons and birds of prey, show regional way of behaving to get their hunting grounds. These regions are basic for keeping a steady food supply.

5.3. Waterfowl: Amphibian Domains

Waterfowl species, including ducks and swans, lay out amphibian domains for settling, raising their young, and getting to assets like sea-going plants and spineless creatures.

Regional Conduct in Warm blooded animals

6.1. Enormous Felines: Savage Domains

Enormous felines, like lions and tigers, are regional hunters. They lay out and protect broad hunting regions that help their rapacious way of life and the endurance of their prides.

6.2. Canids: Social Domains

Canids, including wolves and foxes, frequently structure gatherings with characterized domains. These domains are fundamental for keeping up with bunch attachment, raising posterity, and getting to assets.

6.3. Rodents: Tunnels and Domains

Numerous rat species make tunnels that act as both sanctuary and region. These tunnels are significant for cover, settling, and safeguarding assets like food and water.

Regional Conduct in Amphibian Conditions

7.1. Marine Warm blooded creatures: Maritime Domains

Marine warm blooded creatures, similar to dolphins and seals, lay out domains in the tremendous spans of the sea. These regions act as significant scrounging regions, rearing destinations, and resting areas.

7.2. Coral Reefs: Submerged Land

Fish species possessing coral reefs display regional way of behaving. Regions inside coral reefs offer insurance, sanctuary, and admittance to taking care of justification for these submerged occupants.

7.3. Freshwater Conditions: Stream and Waterway Domains

Freshwater fish, like salmon and trout, lay out domains inside waterways and streams. These domains support their rearing, taking care of, and protecting requirements and are basic for their life cycles.

Covering Domains and Interspecific Collaborations

8.1. Covering Domains

Now and again, creatures share covering domains when assets are plentiful or restricted. These covering regions can prompt helpful or regional resistance conduct.

8.2. Interspecific Regional Sharing

Various species might share regions when their natural specialties and asset necessities don't essentially cover. Interspecific regional connections can limit contest and advance asset dividing.

8.3. Regional Questions

Clashes can emerge when two regional creatures experience each other inside covering ranges. These debates might prompt forceful showdowns, changes in regional limits, or even the relocation of one of the gatherings.

Protection and Moral Contemplations

9.1. Environment Conservation

Understanding regional way of behaving is basic for preservation endeavors. Safeguarding basic natural surroundings guarantees the endurance of regional species by protecting their rearing, taking care of, and shielding regions.

9.2. Untamed life The board

Preservationists and untamed life supervisors use information on regional way of behaving to foster techniques for safeguarding compromised and jeopardized species. These endeavors might incorporate making safeguarded regions, overseeing human-untamed life clashes, and reestablishing territory.

9.3. Moral Contemplations

Preservation endeavors should consider the moral ramifications of upsetting regional creatures or imparting spaces to them. Adjusting human and natural life interests is essential for fruitful concurrence and protection.

4.2 Lorenz's Studies on Territoriality

Konrad Lorenz, the Austrian zoologist and ethologist, made critical commitments to the field of creature conduct, especially in the investigation of territoriality. Lorenz's spearheading work in grasping the systems, capabilities, and ramifications of regional conduct in different creature species shed light on the complexities of social designs and natural transformations. In this 1400-word investigation, we will dive into Lorenz's examinations on territoriality, giving bits of knowledge into his momentous exploration and its persevering through pertinence.

The Groundworks of Ethology

1.1. Ethology: The Investigation of Creature Conduct

Ethology is the logical investigation of creature conduct in normal circumstances. Lorenz was an unmistakable figure in the improvement of ethology, which tries to grasp the development of conduct, the versatile worth of ways of behaving, and the job of correspondence in creature social orders.

1.2. Lorenz's Ethological Approach

Lorenz had faith in the significance of concentrating on creatures in their normal natural surroundings, noticing their ways of behaving and cooperations to acquire bits of knowledge into their social designs and correspondence frameworks. He was a defender of "Konrad Lorenz's engraved geese" as a great representation of ethological research.

1.3. Commitments to the Field

Lorenz's commitments to ethology stretched out past creature conduct. He mentioned significant observable facts on engraving, fixed activity designs, and ethograms, establishing the groundwork for the cutting edge investigation of creature conduct.

Regional Way of behaving as an Ethological Concentration

2.1. Territoriality as a Focal Peculiarity

Lorenz perceived that regional way of behaving was a focal and unavoidable peculiarity in the animals of the world collectively. He comprehended that domains assumed a urgent part in directing asset access, social pecking orders, and regenerative achievement.

2.2. Ethological Perceptions on Territoriality

Lorenz directed broad field perceptions on different creature species, including birds, fish, and vertebrates, to explore regional way of behaving. His fastidious and extensive examinations gave significant bits of knowledge into the instruments and elements of territoriality.

2.3. Key Commitments to Territoriality Exploration

Lorenz's work on the ethology of territoriality exhibited how creatures lay out and keep up with regions, the meaning of regional limits, and the ways of behaving associated with safeguarding and sharing these spaces.

Components of Regional Way of behaving

3.1. Flagging and Correspondence

Lorenz accentuated the job of flagging and correspondence in regional way of behaving. Creatures utilize different signs, including vocalizations, visual presentations, and compound markings, to convey proprietorship, strength, and expectations inside their regions.

3.2. Forceful Collaborations

Lorenz perceived that regional debates frequently include forceful associations. Pecking orders are laid out through conflicts, which effectively decide regional possession and resolve clashes.

3.3. Limit Support

Lorenz's perceptions featured the significance of keeping up with clear regional limits. Creatures utilize visual and olfactory signals to stamp the restrictions of their domains, accordingly lessening the probability of interruptions.

Elements of Regional Way of behaving

4.1. Asset Obtaining and Usage

Lorenz's examinations exhibited that territoriality is firmly connected to asset securing and usage. Creatures guarantee regions to tie down admittance to fundamental assets, including food, water, and safe house.

4.2. Propagation and Settling

Lorenz perceived the job of territoriality in regenerative achievement. Numerous creatures lay out reproducing regions to establish controlled conditions for romance, mating, and raising posterity.

4.3. Guard Against Contenders

Regional way of behaving, as featured by Lorenz, fills in as a guard system against expected contenders. By guaranteeing and shielding regions, creatures lessen the gamble of asset rivalry and disturbance of their day to day exercises.

Regional Conduct in Birds

5.1. Warblers: Vocal and Visual Presentations

Lorenz's perceptions on larks uncovered the significance of vocal and visual showcases in laying out and keeping up with domains. These ways of behaving are fundamental for drawing in mates, preventing rivals, and shielding settling locales.

5.2. Raptors: Savage Regions

Flying predators, like falcons and birds of prey, participate in regional way of behaving to get their hunting grounds. Lorenz's work highlighted the meaning of these domains for keeping a steady food supply.

5.3. Waterfowl: Amphibian Domains

Lorenz's investigations on waterfowl species, including ducks and swans, featured the foundation of amphibian regions for settling, raising youthful, and getting to assets like oceanic plants and spineless creatures.

Regional Conduct in Warm blooded creatures

6.1. Enormous Felines: Ruthless Regions

Lorenz's perceptions of enormous felines, like lions and tigers, displayed their regional conduct in hunting grounds. These regions assume a basic part in keeping a steady food supply and advancing the endurance of prides.

6.2. Canids: Social Regions

Lorenz perceived the regional way of behaving of canids, including wolves and foxes, and their arrangement of gatherings. These regions are critical for keeping up with bunch union, raising posterity, and getting to assets.

6.3. Rodents: Tunnels and Regions

Lorenz's perceptions on rodents, for example, ground squirrels and grassland canines, exhibited their regional way of behaving, which frequently includes the safeguard of tunnels. These tunnels act as haven, settling destinations, and asset security.

Regional Conduct in Amphibian Conditions

7.1. Marine Well evolved creatures: Maritime Domains

Lorenz's examinations on marine well evolved creatures, including dolphins and seals, enlightened their foundation of domains in immense maritime conditions. These regions are fundamental for rummaging, reproducing, and resting.

7.2. Coral Reefs: Submerged Land

Lorenz's perceptions on fish species possessing coral reefs stressed the regional conduct inside these environments. Regions offer security, asylum, and admittance to taking care of justification for these submerged occupants.

7.3. Freshwater Conditions: Stream and Waterway Regions

Lorenz's work on freshwater fish, like salmon and trout, uncovered their regional way of behaving inside waterways and streams. These domains support reproducing, taking care of, and protecting necessities and are vital for their life cycles.

The Heritage and Proceeding with Pertinence

8.1. Lorenz's Persevering through Heritage

Konrad Lorenz's work on territoriality stays powerful in the areas of ethology, creature conduct, and biology. His perceptions have added to how we might interpret the regular world and keep on motivating contemporary examination.

8.2. Future Bearings in Territoriality Studies

Ethologists and specialists expand upon Lorenz's work, utilizing present day research methods and advancements to dive further into the complexities of regional way of behaving. These investigations are fundamental for grasping the developing elements of creature regions.

8.3. Ethological Experiences for Protection

Lorenz's perceptions have functional applications in protection endeavors. Safeguarding environments and understanding regional way of behaving is basic for the protection of jeopardized species and the preservation of biological systems.

4.3 Territorial Strategies in Various Species

Regional way of behaving is a major part of the set of all animals, impacting how creatures interface with their surroundings and conspecifics (individuals from similar species). Across species, regional techniques can differ generally, from the foundation and safeguard of explicit regions to the discussion of shared spaces. In this 1300-word investigation, we will dig into the different regional techniques saw in different species, revealing insight into the components, capabilities, and ramifications of regional way of behaving.

The Groundwork of Regional Techniques

1.1. The Meaning of Regional Procedures

Regional procedures are fundamental for directing asset access, decreasing rivalry, and supporting conceptive achievement. These techniques have advanced as versatile reactions to the natural difficulties looked by changed species.

1.2. Factors Affecting Regional Systems

Different natural and organic variables, like food accessibility, populace thickness, and social designs, impact the turn of events and articulation of regional systems in various species.

1.3. Kinds of Regional Systems

Regional methodologies can envelop a large number of ways of behaving and spatial cases, from savagely safeguarded domains to helpful sharing game plans. The particular techniques rely upon the species' biological specialty and social elements.

Regional Procedures in Birds

2.1. Larks: Overwhelming Protection

Numerous lark species display regional procedures including the lively safeguard of rearing domains. These domains are laid out to draw in mates, secure settling locales, and raise posterity, and they are regularly protected against gatecrashers.

2.2. Raptors: Savage Domains

Raptors, like birds and falcons, lay out regional procedures zeroed in on the guard of hunting grounds. These domains are significant for keeping a steady food supply, as they contain admittance to prey species.

2.3. Frontier Nesters: Agreeable Game plans

Some bird species, similar to penguins and certain seabirds, decide on pilgrim settling. In these cases, people frequently participate and settle in closeness, sharing the weight of hunter protection and chick-raising.

Regional Procedures in Warm blooded animals

3.1. Huge Felines: Prevailing Hunters

Huge carnivores, like lions and tigers, depend on regional procedures to lay out hunting domains. These domains are savagely shielded to guarantee admittance to prey, support prides, and safeguard posterity.

3.2. Canids: Social Domains

Canids, including wolves and foxes, frequently structure gatherings with distinct domains. Social domains assist with keeping up with bunch union, support reproducing, and secure admittance to assets like cave locales and prey.

3.3. Rodents: Tunnels and Predominance

Numerous rat species, similar to ground squirrels and meerkats, use regional techniques that include the guard of tunnels. These tunnels act as both sanctuary and region, giving insurance, settling locales, and asset security.

Regional Procedures in Sea-going Conditions

4.1. Marine Vertebrates: Maritime Domains

Marine well evolved creatures, including dolphins and seals, lay out regional procedures in the tremendous maritime conditions. These regions are crucial for scavenging, resting, and reproducing, as they offer admittance to fundamental assets.

4.2. Coral Reefs: Beautiful People group

Fish species occupying coral reefs frequently show regional procedures. Regional conduct in coral reef environments gives assurance, sanctuary, and admittance to taking care of grounds, adding to the variety and dynamic quality of these submerged networks.

4.3. Freshwater Conditions: Stream and Waterway Regions

Freshwater fish, similar to salmon and trout, utilize regional methodologies inside waterways and streams. These domains support their reproducing, taking care of, and shielding needs and are fundamental for their life cycles.

Regional Methodologies in Friendly Bugs

5.1. Insects: Helpful Domains

Insect provinces take part in regional systems that include agreeable protection of their homes and scrounging regions. This helpful methodology permits insects to get assets and keep up with the honesty of their states.

5.2. Termites: Underground Social orders

Termites show regional systems with regards to underground settlements. These regions are shielded by stations had some expertise in different errands, like scrounging and soldiering, and are urgent for their endurance.

5.3. Honey bees: Hive Regions

Social honey bees, including bumble bees, lay out regional methodologies revolved around hive protection. Hive regions are safeguarded by working drones, and they are fundamental for raising broods, putting away honey, and keeping up with the settlement's honesty.

Covering Domains and Interspecific Associations

6.1. Covering Regions

At times, covering domains are seen when asset accessibility permits it. Regional species might foster agreeable plans that limit clashes and asset contest.

6.2. Interspecific Regional Sharing

Various species might share regions when their environmental specialties and asset prerequisites don't essentially cover. These interspecific regional connections frequently include asset apportioning and shared evasion.

6.3. Regional Questions

Clashes might emerge when two regional creatures experience each other inside covering ranges. These questions can prompt showdowns, changes in regional limits, or the uprooting of one of the gatherings.

Protection and Environmental Ramifications

7.1. Protection Difficulties

Understanding the regional systems of various species is pivotal for powerful protection. Protectionists should think about the effect of natural surroundings misfortune, human infringement, and intrusive species on the regional elements of untamed life.

7.2. Environment Solidness

Regional techniques are necessary to keeping up with the equilibrium and strength of environments. These techniques add to asset guideline, hunter prey elements, and the general strength of environmental networks.

7.3. Moral Contemplations

Adjusting human interests and natural life protection is fundamental while tending to regional species. Moral contemplations ought to direct protection endeavors to limit interruption to creature domains and advance concurrence.

4.4Implications for Understanding Human Societal Structures

The investigation of creature regional way of behaving gives significant bits of knowledge into the activities of the set of all animals as well as human cultural designs. While people have created complex social orders with extraordinary qualities, looking at the regional procedures, correspondence, and social collaborations saw in the collective of animals offers equals and examples that can extend how we might interpret human social orders. In this 1200-word investigation, we will dive into the ramifications of reading up creature regional way of behaving for figuring out human cultural designs, zeroing in on how experiences from the regular world can reveal insight into different parts of human culture.

Regional Way of behaving and Social Ordered progressions

1.1. Territoriality in Creature Social orders

Creature regional way of behaving frequently includes the foundation and guard of domains, which assume a vital part in controlling asset access and keeping up with social orders. These regional frameworks can give bits of knowledge into the human idea of property and asset dissemination.

1.2. Lined up with Property Proprietorship

Human social orders likewise lay out property limits and possession, which reflect the regional cases made by creatures. The acknowledgment of proprietorship and the foundation of property freedoms are major parts of social association in both creature and human social orders.

1.3. Suggestions for Asset Portion

The portion of assets inside creature regions can be connected to the dissemination of assets in human social orders. Understanding how creatures settle asset clashes and oversee asset access can illuminate conversations about asset appropriation in human networks.

Correspondence and Collaboration

2.1. Flagging and Correspondence

Regional creatures utilize different types of correspondence to lay out and keep up with domains. Vocalizations, visual presentations, and synthetic signs pass on data about regional proprietorship, strength, and expectations.

2.2. Illustrations for Human Correspondence

The specialized techniques utilized by creatures can offer experiences into human correspondence inside cultural designs. Viable correspondence is fundamental for settling clashes, laying out friendly pecking orders, and encouraging collaboration, both in creatures and people.

2.3. Collaboration and Compromise

Regional creatures frequently collaborate inside their gatherings to guard domains, raise posterity, and access assets. These helpful endeavors can illuminate conversations about aggregate activities, collective vibes, and compromise methodologies in human social orders.

Covering Domains and Communications

3.1. Covering Domains

In a few creature animal categories, covering domains are seen when assets are plentiful. Helpful or regional resistance conduct limits clashes and asset contest, featuring the advantages of shared spaces.

3.2. Interspecific Regional Sharing

Various species might share regions when their natural specialties and asset necessities don't altogether cover. Examples from interspecific regional sharing can rouse conversations about multicultural social orders and concurrence among different human networks.

3.3. Regional Debates

Clashes might emerge when two regional creatures experience each other inside covering ranges. Bits of knowledge from these regional questions can educate our comprehension regarding clashes between countries, networks, and people in human social orders.

Preservation and Moral Contemplations

4.1. Preservation Difficulties

The investigation of creature regional conduct highlights the meaning of living space safeguarding and protection for the endurance of regional species. Comparable preservation endeavors are urgent for safeguarding the natural surroundings and conditions that help human social orders.

4.2. Environment Steadiness

Regional procedures in the collective of animals add to the equilibrium and dependability of environments. The examples gained from creature associations can feature the significance of keeping up with biological balance in human social orders to guarantee the prosperity of people and networks.

4.3. Moral Contemplations

As we consider protection and concurrence in creature social orders, we should likewise address moral ramifications. The moral contemplations for limiting disturbance to creature regions can act as an aide for tending to moral worries in human social orders, for example, human-untamed life clashes and the freedoms of underestimated populaces.

Cultural Designs and Complex Human Ways of behaving

5.1. Family and Social Units

The social designs saw in creature social orders, which frequently include nuclear families and social progressive systems, have matches in human familial and cultural designs. The association of these designs can give bits of knowledge into the elements of human connections and local area frameworks.

5.2. Financial Frameworks

Examples from asset designation and property proprietorship in creature regions can be applied to human monetary frameworks. Understanding how creatures oversee and disperse assets can illuminate conversations about monetary arrangements, abundance dissemination, and neediness mitigation.

5.3. Administration and Direction

Regional conduct in creatures might uncover administration and dynamic components that resound with human social orders. The techniques creatures use to determine clashes and pursue aggregate choices can offer significant experiences into human administration frameworks, vote based processes, and legitimate structures.

Transformation and Development

6.1. Natural Variation

Regional conduct in the set of all animals is in many cases molded by natural transformation. These variations give bits of knowledge into the capacity of species to flourish in different conditions. Understanding transformation in creatures can illuminate conversations about human variation to changing conditions and cultural difficulties.

6.2. Development of Social Designs

The advancement of regional systems in creatures mirrors the improvement of social designs over the long run. Contrasting the advancement of creature social orders and the authentic improvement of human social orders can yield important bits of knowledge into human social, innovative, and social advancement.

Chapter 5

Mating Rituals and Mate Selection

Mating ceremonies and mate choice are essential parts of the animals of the world collectively, impacting the propagation and endurance of species. These ways of behaving, ceremonies, and procedures have advanced to guarantee the transmission of hereditary material while adjusting to the biological and social settings of every species. In this 2000-word investigation, we will dive into the complexities of mating ceremonies and mate determination, looking at the components, capabilities, and ramifications of these ways of behaving in the regular world.

The Variety of Mating Ceremonies

1.1. Mating Ceremonies as Different Ways of behaving

Mating ceremonies incorporate many ways of behaving and shows. These ceremonies are in many cases species-explicit and can be intricate or basic, contingent upon the biological and social elements of the species.

1.2. Romance Presentations

Romance showcases are a typical part of mating customs, including ways of behaving or actual characteristics that draw in expected mates. These presentations can incorporate vocalizations, moves, and visual shows.

1.3. Regional Way of behaving and Mate Fascination

A few animal categories take part in regional way of behaving as a feature of their mating ceremonies. Shielding and promoting domains can draw in possible mates or lay out predominance.

Components of Mating Customs

2.1. Correspondence and Flagging

Mating ceremonies frequently include complex correspondence and motioning between possible mates. These signs pass on data about the singular's wellbeing, hereditary wellness, and availability to replicate.

2.2. Sexual Determination

Mating ceremonies are molded by the course of sexual determination, where people with specific attributes or ways of behaving are liked as mates. This choice can bring about the advancement of overstated and elaborate mating shows.

2.3. Job of Chemicals

Chemicals assume a critical part in the guideline of mating customs. They impact the timing and power of these ways of behaving and are frequently connected to regenerative cycles and availability.

Mate Choice Models

3.1. Allure and Similarity

Mates are picked in light of their appeal and similarity with the choosing person's necessities. Engaging quality can be affected by actual characteristics, like balance and wellbeing pointers, while similarity includes factors like asset accessibility and conceptive timing.

3.2. Hereditary Similarity

Hereditary similarity is an essential standard for mate choice. Mates are picked in view of their capability to create posterity with great hereditary variety, safe framework similarity, and the capacity to oppose sicknesses.

3.3. Parental Venture

Mate choice can be affected by the normal degree of parental speculation. Guys and females might pick mates who offer the best help and assurance for their posterity.

Mating Customs in Birds

4.1. Warblers: Vocal Exhibitions

Warblers are prestigious for their vocal mating customs, with guys singing complex melodies to draw in females. These melodies pass on data about the vocalist's wellbeing and hereditary wellness.

4.2. Birds of Heaven: Elaborate Presentations

Birds of heaven play out probably the most intricate mating ceremonies in the avian world. Their striking presentations include dynamic plumage, moves, and visual shows to enthrall possible mates.

4.3. Waterfowl: Match Holding

Numerous waterfowl species participate in pair holding customs, where long haul mates structure monogamous bonds. These bonds are many times laid out through romance presentations and vocalizations.

Mating Customs in Warm blooded creatures

5.1. Huge Felines: Predominance and Romance

Huge felines, like lions and tigers, take part in mating customs that incorporate both predominance showcases and romance ways of behaving. These customs guarantee the determination of fit and hereditarily assorted mates.

5.2. Canids: Social Romance

Canids, including wolves and foxes, frequently take part in friendly romance customs. These ways of behaving are pivotal for keeping up with bunch attachment, choosing mates, and supporting the regenerative outcome of the pack.

5.3. Primates: Complex Social Elements

Primates show complex mating ceremonies impacted by their social progressive systems. These customs might include romance presentations, preparing, and predominance associations that guarantee mate determination and keep up with overall vibes.

Mating Ceremonies in Oceanic Conditions

6.1. Marine Well evolved creatures: Melodies of the Sea

Marine warm blooded creatures, like whales and dolphins, are known for their vocal mating ceremonies. These animals utilize complex melodies and vocalizations to impart and draw in mates in the immense maritime climate.

6.2. Coral Reefs: Brilliant Romance

Fish species in coral reefs participate in energetic mating ceremonies, with guys frequently exhibiting elaborate showcases to draw in females. These ceremonies help in the determination of mates and the continuation of species inside the cutthroat reef environment.

6.3. Freshwater Conditions: Settling and Producing

Freshwater fish like salmon and trout show regional and settling ways of behaving. These ceremonies are fundamental for mate choice, generation, and guaranteeing the endurance of posterity in the powerful freshwater climate.

Human Mate Determination

7.1. Social and Social Elements

Human mate choice is impacted by a scope of social and social variables. These variables incorporate social standards, financial status, instruction, and individual inclinations, all of which shape our choices while picking a mate.

7.2. Transformative Brain science

Experiences from creature mating ceremonies are frequently applied to grasping human mate choice. Developmental brain research recommends that people are likewise affected by variables like hereditary variety, wellbeing markers, and conceptive methodologies while choosing mates.

7.3. Changing Elements

Human mate determination is a powerful cycle that develops after some time. Moving social standards, headways in correspondence innovation, and changing social designs impact how people select and connect with possible mates.

Ramifications for Human Cultural Designs

8.1. Social Progressive systems and Match Holding

The complex social progressive systems saw in creature species can measure up to human cultural designs. Understanding pair holding and social pecking orders in the collective of animals can give bits of knowledge into human relational peculiarities and local area association.

8.2. Social Variety and Standards

The job of culture and social variety in human mate choice can be analyzed from the perspective of creature conduct. Social standards and inclinations are not exceptional to people, and they impact mate determination in both creature and human social orders.

8.3. Human Cultural Difficulties

By concentrating on the intricacies of mate determination and mating ceremonies in the set of all animals, we can acquire experiences into a portion of the difficulties and elements present in human social orders. These experiences can illuminate conversations about issues like disparity, variety, and cultural security.

5.1Courtship Behaviors in the Animal Kingdom

Romance ways of behaving in the animals of the world collectively envelop a captivating cluster of ceremonies, showcases, and correspondence systems utilized by people to draw in and select mates. These ways of behaving have advanced as transformations to increment regenerative accomplishment while exploring the natural and social scenes where they happen. In this 1500-word investigation, we will dig into the many-sided universe of romance ways of behaving in the collective of animals, analyzing the systems, capabilities, and ramifications of these ways of behaving in assorted species.

The Variety of Romance Ways of behaving

1.1. Outline of Romance Ways of behaving

Romance ways of behaving are species-explicit and can be astoundingly assorted, going from intricate moves to complex vocalizations and presentations. These ways of behaving are basic for mate determination and regenerative achievement.

1.2. Romance Showcases

Romance frequently includes elaborate presentations, where people grandstand their characteristics or wellness to likely mates. These presentations can incorporate visual, hear-able, or substance components, and they effectively convey data about the singular's allure as an accomplice.

1.3. Job of Regional Way of behaving

Regional way of behaving is in some cases coordinated into romance customs. The guard and show of regions can draw in possible mates and exhibit the singular's capacity to accommodate and safeguard posterity.

Instruments of Romance Ways of behaving

2.1. Correspondence and Flagging

Romance ways of behaving depend intensely on correspondence and flagging. Creatures utilize explicit prompts and motions toward pass on data about their well-being, hereditary wellness, and preparation to replicate to expected mates.

2.2. Sexual Determination

Romance ways of behaving are formed by sexual determination, where people with specific attributes or ways of behaving are liked as mates. This determination cycle can prompt the advancement of overstated and elaborate romance presentations, as well as the improvement of optional sexual qualities.

2.3. Hormonal Guideline

Chemicals assume a huge part in the timing and force of romance ways of behaving. These hormonal changes are frequently connected to regenerative cycles and status to mate, synchronizing the ways of behaving of people inside a populace.

Romance Ways of behaving in Birds

3.1. Larks: Melodic Romance

Larks are famous for their melodic romance ways of behaving. Guys sing complex melodies to draw in females, and the nature of these tunes can pass on data about the vocalist's wellbeing, hereditary wellness, and regional ability.

3.2. Birds of Heaven: Elaborate Showcases

Birds of heaven show probably the most luxurious romance ways of behaving in the avian world. Their striking presentations include lively plumage, perplexing moves, and visual displays pointed toward enamoring expected mates.

3.3. Waterfowl: Match Holding and Vocalizations

Numerous waterfowl species take part in pair holding ceremonies as a feature of their romance ways of behaving. These customs frequently include vocalizations, shared dressing, and synchronized shows, upgrading the connection between likely mates.

Romance Ways of behaving in Warm blooded creatures

4.1. Huge Felines: Predominance and Romance

Huge felines, for example, lions and tigers, consolidate predominance shows with romance ways of behaving. These customs guarantee the choice of fit and hereditarily different mates, as well as the foundation of social progressive systems inside the gathering.

4.2. Canids: Social Romance

Canids, including wolves and foxes, take part in friendly romance ways of behaving that add to keeping up with bunch union and choosing mates. These ways of behaving frequently include play, preparing, and shared support of the social bond.

4.3. Primates: Complex Social Elements

Primates show romance ways of behaving affected by complex social orders. Their ceremonies can incorporate romance presentations, prepping, and predominance collaborations, which assist with guaranteeing mate choice and the support of collective vibes.

Romance Ways of behaving in Sea-going Conditions

5.1. Marine Warm blooded animals: Tunes of the Sea

Marine warm blooded animals, like whales and dolphins, are known for their vocal romance ways of behaving. These animals utilize complex melodies and vocalizations to convey and draw in mates in the huge and frequently dim submerged climate.

5.2. Coral Reefs: Brilliant Romance

Fish species possessing coral reefs participate in lively romance ways of behaving, with guys frequently exhibiting elaborate presentations to draw in females. These customs help in mate choice and the continuation of species inside the cutthroat reef environment.

5.3. Freshwater Conditions: Settling and Bringing forth

Freshwater fish like salmon and trout show regional and settling romance ways of behaving. These ceremonies are fundamental for mate determination, propagation, and guaranteeing the endurance of posterity in the unique freshwater climate.

Ramifications for Human Cultural Designs

6.1. Social Orders and Holding

The complicated social ordered progressions and holding saw in creature romance ways of behaving can be resembled in human social orders. Understanding the job of romance ways of behaving in friendly ordered progressions can give bits of knowledge into human relational peculiarities and local area association.

6.2. Social Variety and Standards

Romance ways of behaving are impacted by social and cultural standards in human social orders. These standards shape human romance customs, inclinations, and assumptions in choosing an accomplice.

6.3. Human Cultural Difficulties

By concentrating on the intricacies of romance ways of behaving in the set of all animals, we can acquire bits of knowledge into a portion of the difficulties and elements present in human social orders. These experiences can illuminate conversations about issues like disparity, variety, and cultural soundness.

5.2 Lorenz's Research on Sexual Selection

Konrad Lorenz was a spearheading ethologist whose exploration on sexual determination gave notable experiences into mate decision and creature conduct. His work contributed essentially to how we might interpret how creatures pick their mates, the job of style in sexual determination, and the advancement of mating inclinations. In this 1400-word investigation, we will dig into Lorenz's original exploration on sexual choice, its suggestions, and its persevering through effect on the area of ethology and transformative science.

The Underpinnings of Ethology

1.1. Ethology as a Discipline

Lorenz was one of the pioneers behind ethology, a field that spotlights on the investigation of creature conduct right at home. He accentuated the significance of noticing creatures in their normal settings to completely figure out their ways of behaving.

1.2. Engraving

Lorenz is maybe generally renowned for his work on engraving, an interaction where youthful creatures structure solid connections to the primary moving item they see, frequently their parent. His perceptions with ducklings and goslings uncovered the complexities of engraving and the basic job of early encounters in profoundly shaping way of behaving.

1.3. The Ethological Way to deal with Sexual Determination

Lorenz's ethological way to deal with sexual determination stressed that creatures settle on decisions about their mates in view of a mix of tangible discernment and previous encounters. His work established the groundwork for grasping the intricacy of mate determination in the animals of the world collectively.

Style and Mate Decision

2.1. The Job of Style

Lorenz's exploration tested the possibility that mate decision was exclusively founded on useful variables like assets and actual wellness. He contended that style assumed a huge part in sexual choice, with creatures choosing mates in light of emotional, stylish inclinations.

2.2. Mate Decision in Birds

Lorenz's investigations of bird species, including peafowls and greylag geese, uncovered the meaning of stylish qualities in mate decision. He saw that extreme presentations, like the beautiful plumage of male peafowls, were liked by females.

2.3. Handicap Guideline

Lorenz's work added to the improvement of the "handicap rule," which recommends that the intricate and exorbitant characteristics showed by guys in romance ceremonies signal their hereditary quality. This standard upset how we might interpret the development of luxurious shows and mate decision.

Lorenz's Questionable Perspectives on Sexual Choice

3.1. Lorenz's Questionable Position

Lorenz's thoughts on sexual determination, especially his accentuation on feel, were met with contention inside mainstream researchers. Numerous analysts had one or two glaring misgivings of his perspectives and the job of feel in mate decision.

3.2. Sexual Choice Returned to

Regardless of the underlying obstruction, Lorenz's commitments to sexual choice have endured everyday hardship. His thoughts regarding style and mate decision have tracked down help in ensuing exploration, showing their persevering through pertinence.

3.3. Effect on Different Fields

Lorenz's exploration has had a significant effect on ethology as well as on fields like brain science, developmental science, and, surprisingly, the investigation of human way of behaving. His experiences keep on molding how we might interpret mate decision and feel in a more extensive setting.

Ramifications and Continuous Exploration

4.1. Preservation and Biodiversity

Lorenz's work on mate decision and sexual choice has basic ramifications for preservation endeavors. Understanding the variables that drive mate decision can illuminate procedures to safeguard biodiversity and safeguard imperiled species.

4.2. Developmental Science

Lorenz's exploration has affected the investigation of developmental science, especially with regards to speciation and the broadening of characteristics through sexual choice. His thoughts keep on being pertinent in the examination of how species develop and adjust.

4.3. Human Way of behaving and Mate Decision

Lorenz's work on style in mate decision has matches in human way of behaving and inclinations in choosing mates. His bits of knowledge can be applied to the investigation of human mate choice and the job of appeal in close connections.

5.3 Factors Influencing Mate Choice

Mate decision is a basic part of generation in the set of all animals. It includes the determination of an accomplice for mating, a choice impacted by a mix of organic, mental, and transformative variables. Understanding the components behind mate decision is significant for revealing insight into the variety of regenerative systems saw in nature. In this 1300-word investigation, we will dive into the complex universe of elements that impact mate decision, from hereditary qualities and tactile discernment to social and ecological factors.

Organic Variables

1.1. Hereditary Similarity

Hereditary similarity assumes a critical part in mate decision. Creatures frequently pick mates with hereditary attributes that supplement their own, prompting expanded hereditary variety in their posterity. This variety can upgrade protection from infections and versatility to evolving conditions.

1.2. Immunogenetic Similarity

The significant histocompatibility complex (MHC) is a hereditary variable that impacts mate decision. Creatures, including people, are more drawn to people with MHC qualities not the same as their own. This inclination might be connected with a superior safe framework and sickness opposition in posterity.

1.3. Fruitfulness and Conceptive Wellness

People frequently select mates in view of signs connected with fruitfulness and conceptive wellness. These prompts can incorporate actual qualities that imply great wellbeing, high energy levels, and a solid capacity to repeat.

Tangible Insight

2.1. Viewable Signs

Obvious prompts are an essential calculate mate decision. The presence of possible mates, including their actual elements, tinge, and shows, can significantly impact a singular's choice to pick a mate. Brilliant varieties, evenness, and elaborate presentations are frequently liked.

2.2. Hear-able Signs

Hear-able signs, like vocalizations and tunes, are urgent in mate decision for some species. The quality, intricacy, and consistency of these vocalizations can give data about the mate's wellbeing, hereditary wellness, and accessibility.

2.3. Olfactory and Substance Signs

Olfactory prompts, including pheromones, assume a huge part in mate decision for certain creatures. These synthetic signs can pass on data about the mate's regenerative status, hereditary similarity, and societal position.

Mental and Mental Elements

3.1. Character and Similarity

Creatures frequently evaluate the character and similarity of possible mates. This assessment incorporates factors like social way of behaving, personality, and the capacity to cooperate in nurturing and other agreeable exercises.

3.2. Learning and Memory

Learning and memory assume a part in mate decision, as people might recall effective or fruitless communications with expected mates. These encounters can impact future choices about mate determination.

3.3. Individual Inclinations

Individual inclinations for explicit attributes or ways of behaving can likewise impact mate decision. These inclinations might be impacted by early encounters, social variables, or individual tendencies, prompting variety in mate decisions even inside an animal categories.

Natural and Environmental Variables

4.1. Asset Accessibility

Natural elements, like the accessibility of assets, can shape mate decision. In species where guys give assets to females or posterity, females might pick mates with admittance to bountiful assets.

4.2. Predation Hazard

The gamble of predation can influence mate decision. Now and again, people might favor mates that lessen their weakness to hunters, regardless of whether these mates have the most appealing characteristics.

4.3. Environmental Specialties and Transformation

Mate decision is likewise affected by environmental specialties. Species adjust to their surroundings, and mate decision can mirror this transformation. For instance, species living in unforgiving conditions might focus on qualities that upgrade endurance and multiplication.

Social and Social Elements

5.1. Social Orders

Social orders and the situation with people inside a gathering can influence mate decision. In species with prevailing pecking orders, high-positioning people might have more prominent admittance to mates, influencing the conveyance of accomplices.

5.2. Social Standards and Customs

Social standards and customs impact mate decision in people and a few creature social orders. These standards direct OK accomplices in light of variables like age, social class, and religion, and they can shift generally between societies.

5.3. Social Learning

Social learning can shape mate decision through perception and impersonation of others in the gathering. Youthful people might gain from the decisions and ways of behaving of more established, more experienced people.

Transformative Ramifications

6.1. Coevolution of Qualities

Mate decision is a significant driver of transformative change. Individuals decisions can prompt the development of explicit characteristics, like tinge, size, and conduct shows. This coevolution among inclinations and qualities can bring about the variety of species saw in the regular world.

6.2. Conceptive Techniques

Mate decision is firmly connected to the development of regenerative techniques. Various species show different regenerative strategies, like monogamy, polygyny, and polyandry, which have advanced because of mate decision and the biological setting.

6.3. Species Disparity and Speciation

Mate decision can prompt species disparity and speciation. At the point when people reliably pick mates with explicit qualities or from specific populaces, it can bring about regenerative confinement and the arrangement of new species.

5.4Lessons from Animal Mating for Human Relationships

Human connections, especially those of a heartfelt sort, have for quite some time been the subject of interest and study. While human collaborations are without a doubt complex, we can draw important experiences from the universe of creature mating to all the more likely figure out affection, fascination, and similarity. In this 1200-word investigation, we will dig into the examples that creature mating can propose for human connections, from the job of style and mate decision to the significance of correspondence and responsibility.

The Job of Style and Fascination

1.1. Style in Mate Decision

Creatures frequently pick mates in light of style, and people are no special case. Actual engaging quality and visual allure assume a huge part in both creature and human mate choice.

1.2. The Effect of Evenness

Evenness is a vital calculate engaging quality for some species, including people. Concentrates on show that people with even facial highlights are frequently seen as more alluring, which can impact starting fascination.

1.3. Social Fluctuation

Social standards and goals of magnificence shape human view of engaging quality. These social inclinations can vary broadly, underscoring the impact of society on our thoughts of what is alluring.

Correspondence and Romance

2.1. Vocalizations and Articulation

Creature romance frequently includes vocalizations and expressive ways of behaving that effectively impart interest and fascination. Additionally, correspondence is vital in human connections, assisting people with communicating their sentiments, expectations, and wants.

2.2. Ceremonies and Showcases

Romance customs and presentations in the collective of animals should be visible as types of non-verbal correspondence. People additionally take part in non-verbal signs, for example, non-verbal communication, eye to eye connection, and actual touch, to convey their feelings and fascination.

2.3. Similarity and Consistency

Consistency in correspondence is fundamental. Similarly as creatures search for signals that reliably convey interest, people esteem accomplices who impart transparently, reliably, and genuinely to construct trust in their connections.

Responsibility and Long haul Pair Bonds

3.1. Monogamy in Creatures

A few creature animal varieties structure long haul monogamous bonds, underscoring responsibility as a fundamental part of effective mating. In the human setting, monogamy and responsibility are essential to the development of enduring connections.

3.2. The Job of Trust

Trust is essential in keeping a solid relationship, whether in the set of all animals or among people. Laying out trust is in many cases a consequence of predictable way of behaving, clear correspondence, and shared regard.

3.3. Challenges in Long haul Responsibility

Long haul responsibility can confront difficulties, including the need to adjust and become together. The capacity to explore life changes and adjust to new conditions is critical to the outcome of both creature pair bonds and human connections.

The Significance of Similarity

4.1. Hereditary Similarity

A creature animal categories focus on hereditary similarity to guarantee the well-being and endurance of their posterity. While human similarity isn't exclusively founded on hereditary qualities, it assumes a part in our fascination with expected accomplices.

4.2. Shared Interests and Values

Similarity in human connections reaches out to shared interests, values, and life objectives. The arrangement of these variables can encourage congruity and lessen clashes in connections.

4.3. Versatility and Adaptability

The capacity to adjust and be adaptable in light of changing conditions is significant in both creature and human connections. Similarity frequently depends on an accomplice's ability to adjust to developing requirements and difficulties.

Mating Techniques and Methodologies for Adoration

5.1. Variety in Mating Techniques

Creature mating techniques are assorted, going from monogamy to polygamy and in the middle between. Human connections likewise display a wide range of procedures, from long lasting monogamy to open connections, mirroring our adaptability and flexibility.

5.2. The Impact of Development

Development has formed both creature mating procedures and human connections. Examples from the animals of the world collectively stress the significance of transformation and the potential for assorted mating methodologies.

5.3. Respecting Individual Decision

Similarly as creatures pursue individual decisions in view of their requirements and conditions, human connections ought to respect individual decisions and necessities. This can cultivate better, additional satisfying associations.

Chapter 6

Parental Care and Offspring Rearing

Parental consideration and posterity raising are basic parts of everyday life in the animals of the world collectively. These ways of behaving are not select to people but rather are seen across many species, each with its one of a kind variations to guarantee the endurance and prosperity of their posterity. In this 2000-word investigation, we will dig into the captivating universe of parental consideration and posterity raising, looking at the variety of systems, the elements that impact them, and the ramifications for figuring out relational peculiarities, advancement, and, surprisingly, human nurturing.

The Variety of Parental Consideration

1.1. Outline of Parental Consideration

Parental consideration alludes to the ways of behaving showed by guardians to guarantee the endurance, development, and improvement of their posterity. It can include different exercises, from giving food and asylum to security and direction.

1.2. Kinds of Parental Consideration

Parental consideration procedures fluctuate generally among species. They can be ordered into various kinds, including maternal consideration, fatherly consideration, and biparental care, each including various levels of speculation and obligations.

1.3. Outrageous Parental Consideration

A few animal types display outrageous types of parental consideration, for example, egg agonizing, mouth agonizing, and delayed nursing. These transformations are significant for the endurance of posterity and give knowledge into the advancement of complicated ways of behaving.

The Variables Impacting Parental Consideration

2.1. Asset Accessibility

The accessibility of assets, like food, assumes a huge part in forming parental consideration methodologies. In conditions with plentiful assets, guardians might put more in generation, while in asset scant settings, they could embrace various methodologies.

2.2. Predation Hazard

The degree of predation risk additionally impacts parental consideration. In regions with high predation pressure, guardians might put more in defensive measures, while those in more secure conditions can distribute assets in an unexpected way.

2.3. Conceptive Procedures

Different conceptive procedures, for example, the quantity of posterity created, can influence parental consideration. Species that produce less posterity frequently put additional significant investment into every one, while those with numerous posterity might give less consideration per posterity.

Parental Consideration in the Avian World

3.1. Birds: Home Structure and Taking care of

Avian species show an extensive variety of parental consideration ways of behaving. A few birds are known for their fastidious home structure, while others are famous for their disgorging of food to take care of their posterity.

3.2. Altricial versus Precocial Posterity

Birds can have altricial (defenseless) or precocial (more free) posterity. The degree of parental consideration gave frequently relates to the formative phase of the youthful, with altricial posterity requiring more consideration and taking care of.

3.3. Agreeable Rearing

Agreeable rearing, where different people assist with raising the posterity, is seen in different bird species. These agreeable endeavors can include kin, irrelevant people, or even individuals from a similar sex.

Parental Consideration in Warm blooded creatures

4.1. Vertebrates: Nursing and Assurance

Well evolved creatures display a different scope of parental consideration ways of behaving, including nursing, prepping, and security. The mammalian connection among mother and posterity is frequently serious areas of strength for especially.

4.2. Marsupials: Pockets and Kangaroo Care

Marsupials have exceptional techniques for parental consideration, with females conveying their immature posterity in pockets. Kangaroo care, where the youthful are carried on the parent's body, is a notable illustration of marsupial consideration.

4.3. Monogamous Warm blooded animals

A few monogamous warm blooded creatures, like beavers and wolves, take part in biparental care. The two guardians cooperate to give food, assurance, and haven for their posterity, exhibiting collaboration in raising the youthful.

Parental Consideration in Fish

5.1. Fish: Home Structure and Protecting

Fish species display different parental consideration methodologies. Some form homes for their eggs, while others watch their posterity from hunters. These ways of behaving can be impacted by factors like water temperature and predation risk.

5.2. Mouth Brooders

Some fish, similar to cichlids, are mouth brooders, where one or the two guardians safeguard and convey their young in their mouths. This type of parental consideration gives a protected climate to the weak posterity.

5.3. Agreeable Nurturing

Agreeable nurturing is likewise seen in fish, with various people from similar gathering or species assisting with really focusing on and safeguard the youthful. This common obligation can upgrade the endurance of the posterity.

The Advancement of Parental Consideration

6.1. Transformative Compromises

The development of parental consideration frequently includes compromises between interest in current posterity and expected future multiplication. The harmony between parental speculation and individual conceptive wellness shapes the advancement of parental consideration procedures.

6.2. Wellness Advantages

Parental consideration can give critical wellness benefits, like expanded posterity endurance and upgraded admittance to mates. These advantages add to the advancement and constancy of parental consideration ways of behaving.

6.3. Coevolution of Parental Consideration

The coevolution of parental consideration ways of behaving and posterity attributes is a fundamental part of the development of day to day life. As posterity advance to more readily take advantage of parental consideration, guardians foster procedures to safeguard their ventures.

Ramifications for Grasping Human Nurturing

7.1. Human Nurturing as a Continuation

Human nurturing imparts similitudes to creature parental consideration, as both include accommodating, safeguarding, and supporting posterity. Understanding the advancement and variety of parental consideration in the collective of animals can reveal insight into the beginnings of human nurturing ways of behaving.

7.2. Social Changeability

Social standards and cultural designs impact human nurturing, similar as natural elements shape creature parental consideration. Social changeability in human nurturing rehearses features the flexibility of nurturing ways of behaving.

7.3. Illustrations from Creature Nurturing

Illustrations from creature nurturing ways of behaving can give bits of knowledge into parts of human nurturing, like the significance of asset accessibility, the job of collaboration, and the advancement of connection and holding among guardians and posterity.

6.1 The Bonds Between Parents and Offspring

The connections among guardians and their posterity are probably the most significant and complex connections in human life. These associations are not restricted to organic ties but rather stretch out to new parents, gatekeepers, and even coaches who assume a significant part in deeply shaping the existences of the more youthful age. The parent-posterity bond is an unpredictable interaction of science, brain research, and culture, and it significantly impacts the turn of events and prosperity of people. In this 1500-word investigation, we will dive into the complex idea of these bonds, analyzing their natural establishments, mental aspects, and social varieties, while likewise thinking about the ramifications for self-improvement and cultural elements.

Organic Underpinnings of Parent-Posterity Bonds

At its center, the parent-posterity bond has natural underpinnings that have advanced north of millions of years. These natural establishments are especially obvious in warm blooded creatures, where maternal consideration is a basic part of posterity endurance. In people, the bonds are not restricted to moms but rather stretch out to fathers and different parental figures. The natural premise of these bonds incorporates:

Connection and Reliance: From the snapshot of birth, newborn children are naturally wired to look for vicinity and connection to their guardians. This connection guarantees the endurance and prosperity of the posterity, as they depend on their folks for food, insurance, and consistent reassurance.

The demonstration of breastfeeding, for example, discharges oxytocin, a chemical that develops the maternal bond and upgrades the connection among mother and kid.

Hereditary Engraving: Hereditary elements assume a critical part in parent-posterity bonds. Kids acquire a mix of qualities from their folks, which can impact different parts of their turn of events, including actual characteristics, defenselessness to specific infections, and even character attributes. This hereditary association supports the feeling of character and having a place inside the family.

Hormonal Guideline: Chemicals, like oxytocin and vasopressin, are complicatedly engaged with fortifying the connection among guardians and posterity. These chemicals are delivered during actual contact and close to home connections, adding to sensations of affection and connection. They assist guardians with holding with their kids, guaranteeing their consideration and assurance.

Mental Elements of Parent-Posterity Bonds

While the natural establishments give the underlying force to parent-posterity bonds, the mental aspects are similarly fundamental in molding these connections. The accompanying elements add to the intricacy of these bonds:

Close to home Connection: Profound connection is a foundation of parent-posterity connections. It is described by sensations of adoration, friendship, and a profound feeling of obligation for the prosperity of one's youngsters. This connection frequently stretches out past youth and endures all through the life expectancy, making a long lasting association.

Job Demonstrating: Guardians assume a significant part in molding the qualities, convictions, and ways of behaving of their youngsters. Kids frequently focus on their folks as good examples and are intensely impacted by their folks' mentalities and activities. This job demonstrating lastingly affects a singular's turn of events and personality.

Support and Sustaining: Guardians give close to home, social, and monetary help to their posterity, which is imperative for their development and advancement. This help isn't restricted to addressing fundamental necessities yet in addition incorporates direction, support, and a place of refuge for individual investigation.

Connection Styles: The nature of parent-posterity bonds can impact a singular's connection style, which, thus, influences their connections in adulthood. Secure connections commonly result from responsive and sustaining nurturing, while shaky connections might originate from conflicting or careless providing care.

Social Varieties in Parent-Posterity Bonds

Parent-posterity bonds are formed by science and brain research as well as by social standards and values. The idea of these connections can differ fundamentally starting with one culture then onto the next. A few key social varieties include:

Obedient Devotion in Confucian Societies: In numerous Asian societies impacted by Confucianism, there is major areas of strength for an on dutiful devotion, where youngsters are supposed to extend profound regard and unwaveringness to their folks. This social standard puts a high worth on the parent-posterity bond and frequently incorporates a feeling of obligation and commitment towards one's folks.

Independence in Western Societies: Western social orders will generally focus on independence and freedom. While parent-posterity bonds are as yet huge, there is much of the time a more prominent accentuation on private independence and the quest for individual objectives. This can prompt a more independent way to deal with adulthood and less relationship inside families.

More distant families versus Family units: Social standards additionally impact the construction of families. In certain societies, for example, in numerous African and Center Eastern social orders, more distant families assume a conspicuous part in youngster raising and backing. Conversely, Western societies frequently favor family units, prompting various elements in parent-posterity bonds.

Suggestions for Self-awareness and Cultural Elements

The strength and nature of parent-posterity bonds have extensive ramifications for self-improvement and cultural elements. These connections can impact a singular's confidence, personal prosperity, and by and large life fulfillment. They can likewise influence more extensive cultural issues, like social union and generational coherence.

Self-awareness: A solid and strong parent-posterity bond can add to a youngster's personal prosperity and confidence. It gives an underpinning of safety from which people can investigate and foster their own personalities. Alternately, stressed or broken connections might bring about profound trouble and impede self-awareness.

Relationship and Social Union: Solid parent-posterity bonds can cultivate a feeling of reliance and shared help inside families. These securities can stretch out to more extensive networks, advancing social union and interconnectedness.

Generational Coherence: Parent-posterity bonds likewise assume a basic part in the congruity of social customs, values, and information across ages. Passing down family backgrounds, customs, and values is a fundamental part of keeping up with social personality.

Life as a parent and Providing care: As people become guardians themselves, the nature of their own parent-posterity bonds frequently impacts their nurturing style and approach. Positive encounters can prompt seriously sustaining and strong nurturing, while negative encounters might prompt difficulties in giving a sound climate to their own youngsters.

Difficulties and Changes in Current culture

In current culture, different elements have achieved changes and difficulties in parent-posterity bonds. A portion of these include:

Balance between serious and fun activities: The requests of present day life, including long work hours and occupied plans, can once in a while make it trying for guardians to invest quality energy with their youngsters. Accomplishing a harmony among work and day to day life is difficult for some guardians.

Innovation and Online Entertainment: The coming of innovation and web-based entertainment has brought new elements into parent-posterity connections. Guardians and kids frequently battle with screen time, cyberbullying, and the effect of advanced correspondence on their connections.

Moving Orientation Jobs: Developing orientation jobs imply that the two guardians are presently bound to be participated in both providing care and work. This shift can prompt more evenhanded nurturing liabilities yet in addition requires transformation and correspondence inside families.

Maturing Populace: With expanded future, numerous grown-ups end up in the job of really focusing on their maturing guardians while as yet supporting their own kids. This "sandwich age" peculiarity presents special difficulties in overseeing providing care liabilities.

6.2 Lorenz's Findings on Parental Behavior

Konrad Lorenz, an Austrian ethologist, made huge commitments to the field of creature conduct and the comprehension of parental way of behaving. His spearheading work on engraving and the natural systems overseeing parental consideration in creatures shed light on the unpredictable universe of providing care in both the collective of animals and human social orders. This investigation digs into Lorenz's striking discoveries, zeroing in on his examination on engraving, the basic time frame idea, and the ramifications of his work for figuring out parental conduct in the more extensive setting.

Engraving and Its Importance

Engraving is a peculiarity that Lorenz broadly considered, zeroing in on the basic period during which it happens. Engraving is the quick and irreversible connection that happens between a youthful creature and the main moving item it experiences, frequently its mom or a proxy. Lorenz's momentous exploration during the 1930s, essentially led on waterfowl like geese and ducks, revealed a few critical parts of engraving:

Basic Period: Lorenz found that engraving is profoundly time-touchy, happening during a particular "basic period" not long after incubating. This basic period is an open door for the youthful creature to frame an enduring bond with the article it experiences. The timing fluctuates across species, however it is commonly in the initial not many hours or long periods of life.

Irreversibility: Whenever engraving has happened, it is basically irreversible. The bond shaped during this cycle is strong and enduring, influencing the creature's social ways of behaving and affiliations all through its life.

Species-Explicit: Engraving is species-explicit, implying that creatures will generally engrave on conspecifics (individuals from their own species). Notwithstanding, Lorenz's examination additionally showed the chance of engraving on non-conspecifics under specific circumstances.

Lorenz's discoveries on engraving have huge ramifications for grasping parental conduct in creatures. It features the significance of early cooperations and providing care in forming the social connections and affiliations of creatures. Engraving can impact mate determination, relocation examples, and social orders, among different parts of a creature's life.

The Ethological Viewpoint on Parental Consideration

Lorenz's work on engraving and parental way of behaving added to the improvement of ethology, a part of science that spotlights on the investigation of creature conduct in normal settings. Ethologists like Lorenz stressed the significance of noticing creatures in their regular environments and figuring out their conduct in biological and transformative settings. This approach took into consideration a more profound comprehension of the inborn components and versatile elements of parental consideration.

Key bits of knowledge according to Lorenz's ethological point of view on parental consideration include:

Inborn Ways of behaving: Lorenz contended that numerous parts of parental consideration, for example, securing and taking care of posterity, are intrinsic ways of behaving driven by hereditary variables. These ways of behaving are much of the time present even without any related knowledge or learning.

Fixed Activity Examples: Ethologists proposed the idea of "fixed activity designs," which are generalized, untaught ways of behaving that are set off by unambiguous boosts. With regards to parental consideration, these examples incorporate home structure, taking care of, prepping, and safeguarding posterity.

Versatile Capabilities: Ethologists like Lorenz accepted that parental consideration has versatile capabilities, guaranteeing the endurance and conceptive outcome of posterity. The explicitness and adequacy of these ways of behaving, frequently impacted by engraving, add to the posterity's prosperity.

Human Ramifications

While Lorenz's work basically centered around creatures, the experiences acquired from his exploration have suggestions for grasping parental conduct in people. Human nurturing is an intricate exchange of natural, mental, and social elements, yet certain parts of Lorenz's discoveries can be applied to how we might interpret human parental way of behaving:

Early Connection: Lorenz's idea of a basic period lines up with the possibility of early connection in human babies. Connection hypothesis, created by John Bowlby, highlights the significance of the guardian baby bond during the initial not many long periods of life, which can lastingly affect a kid's personal and social turn of events.

Parent-Kid Holding: Lorenz's accentuation on the irreversibility of engraving proposes that early parent-kid cooperations can lastingly affect a kid's connection to their folks. This connection, thus, impacts the kid's social and close to home turn of events.

Social Variety: Similarly as engraving can fluctuate across species, nurturing rehearses likewise display social varieties in human social orders. Various societies have unmistakable standards and assumptions about parental jobs and providing care works on, affecting the parent-kid bond.

Difficulties and Debates

Lorenz's work, however historic, has confronted analysis and discussions throughout the long term. A portion of the difficulties to his discoveries and their suggestions include:

Moral Worries: Engraving probes creatures, as directed by Lorenz and others, have raised moral worries. The detachment of youthful creatures from their normal guardians and openness to fake upgrades for research purposes affects the creatures' prosperity.

Misrepresentation: Pundits contend that Lorenz's accentuation on natural ways of behaving and fixed activity examples might distort the intricacy of parental consideration, both in creatures and people. Human nurturing, specifically, is impacted by an extensive variety of social, social, and natural factors that go past inborn ways of behaving.

Restricted Pertinence: The idea of engraving, with its emphasis on early-educational encounters, may not completely represent the scope of variables that impact human nurturing and youngster improvement. In human social orders, factors like social practices, financial status, and nurturing styles assume critical parts.

6.3 Strategies for Successful Offspring Rearing

Effective posterity raising is a key part of human and creature life, fundamental for the continuation of species and the prosperity of people in the future. The methodologies utilized for raising posterity are assorted and complex, affected by organic, mental, and social variables. This investigation dives into different systems for effective posterity raising, analyzing the standards and practices that guide the sustaining of kids in various settings and their suggestions for self-improvement and cultural prosperity.

Natural Groundworks of Posterity Raising

The natural basic for posterity raising is established in the propagation of qualities and species endurance. Natural factors altogether shape the procedures for effective posterity raising, and these include:

Maternal Nature: In numerous species, females show maternal impulses driven by hormonal changes during pregnancy and after birth. These impulses lead moms to give care and insurance to their posterity, guaranteeing their endurance and prosperity.

Parental Speculation: The idea of parental venture, as proposed by Robert Trivers, recognizes that raising posterity demands significant investment, energy, and assets. Guardians assign these speculations to expand the possibilities of their posterity's endurance and regenerative achievement.

Hereditary Legacy: Posterity acquire qualities from their folks, affecting different attributes, including physical, scholarly, and social qualities. Hereditary legacy assumes a pivotal part in the transmission of characteristics across ages.

Mental Components of Posterity Raising

Past science, the methodologies for fruitful posterity raising are additionally well established in mental angles. These aspects shape the parent-youngster relationship, influence the kid's personal turn of events, and impact nurturing rehearses:

Connection Hypothesis: Connection hypothesis, created by John Bowlby, accentuates the significance of the early parent-kid bond. A solid connection during outset and youth is related with profound prosperity, flexibility, and the capacity to frame sound connections in later life.

Nurturing Styles: Different nurturing styles, for example, legitimate, tyrant, lenient, and careless, particularly affect youngsters' turn of events. Nurturing rehearses impact a kid's way of behaving, confidence, and capacity to adapt to difficulties.

Social Variety: Social standards and values altogether impact nurturing techniques. Various societies have unmistakable convictions and practices connected with kid raising, including discipline, instruction, and orientation jobs.

Techniques for Fruitful Posterity Raising

Effective posterity raising includes a huge number of methodologies and practices that help the physical, profound, and scholarly improvement of kids. A few key procedures include:

Profound Sustaining: Offering close to home help and a protected connection is fundamental. Youngsters flourish when they feel adored, esteemed, and protected in their family climate. Profound supporting adds to solid confidence and close to home prosperity.

Sustenance and Medical services: Guaranteeing youngsters get legitimate nourishment and medical care is basic to their actual turn of events. An even eating routine and normal clinical check-ups are vital for development and prosperity.

Training and Scholarly Feeling: Giving youngsters admittance to schooling and scholarly excitement is fundamental for mental turn of events. Youth training, perusing, and openness to various encounters advance scholarly development.

Discipline and Limits: Defining proper limits and utilizing positive discipline techniques is significant for showing youngsters conduct and results. Compelling discipline strategies assist kids with creating restraint and compassion.

Empowering Freedom: Cultivating freedom is fundamental for a kid's confidence and improvement. Permitting kids to pursue age-fitting choices and take on liabilities fabricates their certainty and critical thinking abilities.

Social and Moral Qualities: Passing on social and moral qualities is a significant part of posterity raising. These qualities give an ethical structure to kids, assisting them with exploring moral problems and pursue dependable decisions.

Cultural and Social Ramifications

Systems for fruitful posterity raising have significant ramifications for society and culture. The prosperity of youngsters and their improvement straightforwardly impact the general wellbeing and soundness of a local area or society. A few key ramifications include:

Social Union: A general public with fruitful posterity raising practices will in general have more grounded social union, as kids grow up with a feeling of having a place and association with their networks.

Financial Efficiency: All around sustained kids are bound to become useful, contributing citizenry. They are better prepared to seek after schooling and vocations, helping the economy.

Social Coherence: Passing on social customs and values through posterity raising guarantees the progression of a culture. These practices are safeguarded and conveyed forward by the more youthful age.

Social Issues: Deficient posterity raising can prompt different social issues, including adolescent wrongdoing, psychological wellness issues, and a higher probability of taking part in dangerous ways of behaving.

Difficulties and Variations

Fruitful posterity raising isn't without its difficulties and transformations. The techniques utilized by guardians might have to develop in light of changing social and natural circumstances. A few difficulties include:

Mechanical Impacts: The impact of innovation and screen time on nurturing and youngster improvement is a cutting edge challenge. Guardians should adjust to explore the effect of advanced media on their youngsters' lives.

Balance between fun and serious activities: Adjusting work and everyday life can be really difficult for guardians, influencing how much time and consideration they can commit to their youngsters.

Social Movements: As social orders advance, social standards and values connected with posterity raising might change. Transformation to these movements is fundamental for guaranteeing that nurturing rehearses line up with the advancing requirements of youngsters and society.

Monetary Tensions: Financial tensions can influence the assets accessible to guardians for kid raising. Financial incongruities can prompt inconsistent open doors for youngsters' development and improvement.

6.4 Comparative Insights into Human Parenting

Human nurturing is a complicated and multi-layered try, formed by a blend of organic, mental, and social elements. To acquire a more profound comprehension of human nurturing, we can focus on similar experiences from the set of all animals. Noticing nurturing ways of behaving in different species offers significant viewpoints on the central parts of nurturing, including providing care, security, and socialization. In this investigation, we will look at near experiences into human nurturing, taking into account the two shared traits and contrasts in nurturing systems among different species.

Organic Groundworks of Nurturing

Nurturing in the animals of the world collectively and among people shares normal natural establishments that are attached in the drive to guarantee the endurance and prosperity of posterity. These establishments include:

Parental Speculation: Parental venture hypothesis, as proposed by Robert Trivers, recommends that guardians allot assets to expand their posterity's possibilities of endurance and generation. This idea is applicable to the two people and creatures, underscoring the responsibility and penances guardians make for their kids.

Connection Systems: Connection is a central part of nurturing across species. In people, connection hypothesis, as evolved by John Bowlby, underscores the significance of the parent-youngster bond. Comparative connection components can be seen in creature species, where youthful creatures structure bonds with their guardians to guarantee assurance and admittance to assets.

Hereditary Legacy: Posterity acquire qualities from their folks, affecting different attributes, including physical, mental, and conduct qualities. The transmission of hereditary data is a shared characteristic shared by all species, including people.

Mental Components of Nurturing

While natural variables give the establishment to nurturing, mental aspects assume a basic part in forming nurturing ways of behaving. These aspects are educated by the species' particular necessities and social designs. A few key mental perspectives include:

Parent-Kid Bond: The connection among guardians and their posterity is integral to nurturing. In people, connection hypothesis features the meaning of early parent-kid bonds in profound turn of events. Essentially, in the animals of the world collectively, the parent-posterity bond is basic for the endurance and prosperity of youthful.

Nurturing Styles: The two people and creatures display varieties in nurturing styles. In people, these styles incorporate definitive, tyrant, tolerant, and careless nurturing. In the animals of the world collectively, contrasts in nurturing systems can be seen among species, like birds, well evolved creatures, and bugs, in light of their biological and social settings.

Learning and Socialization: Nurturing frequently includes instructing and mingling posterity. In people, this incorporates bestowing social standards and values. In creatures, the most common way of showing youthful how to track down food, perceive dangers, and explore their current circumstance is fundamental for their endurance.

Similar Bits of knowledge from Animals of the world collectively

By looking at nurturing ways of behaving in different creature species, we can acquire significant bits of knowledge into human nurturing. A few essential models include:

Vertebrates: Warm blooded animals, similar to people, put huge time and assets in nurturing. Numerous warm blooded creatures give sustenance through breastfeeding, care for their posterity, and deal insurance. The profound bonds shaped among mother and youngster in numerous mammalian species equal the connection found in people.

Birds: Avian nurturing offers experiences into the variety of nurturing ways of behaving. For instance, monogamous bird species frequently share nurturing obligations, with the two guardians adding to hatching and chick-raising. This agreeable nurturing looks like shared nurturing liabilities saw in human families.

Bugs: Social bugs like insects and honey bees show the significance of division of work in nurturing. Sovereigns and laborer insects are answerable for laying eggs and keeping an eye on the youthful, reflecting the progressive design saw in a few human social orders.

Fish: Some fish species show interesting nurturing ways of behaving, for example, mouthbrooding. Male fish convey treated eggs in their mouths, giving security and oxygenation until the fry are prepared to swim all alone. This type of care matches the human job of fathers in providing care.

Human-Explicit Parts of Nurturing

While there are numerous shared characteristics in nurturing across species, people display a few remarkable viewpoints that separate their nurturing rehearses:

Social Variety: Human nurturing is exceptionally impacted by culture. Various social orders have unmistakable nurturing standards, values, and assumptions. Social practices, like transitional experiences, services, and nurturing styles, essentially shape human nurturing ways of behaving.

Moral and Moral Instruction: Not at all like most creature species, people give moral and moral training to their posterity. Guardians show their youngsters values, morals, and social standards, setting them up for moral direction and dependable way of behaving.

Complex Mental Turn of events: Human youngsters go through broad mental turn of events, including language obtaining, critical thinking abilities, and dynamic reasoning. Nurturing in people includes addressing essential requirements as well as supporting scholarly and close to home development.

Broadened Nurturing Period: People have a lengthy time of reliance, with youngsters requiring care and direction for a drawn out term. Dissimilar to numerous creature species where posterity become autonomous moderately rapidly, human nurturing goes on for a very long time.

Difficulties and Variations

Human nurturing faces various moves and requires continuous transformations to changing cultural and ecological circumstances. A portion of the difficulties include:

Mechanical Impacts: Present day innovation, especially advanced media, has modified nurturing rehearses. Guardians should adjust to explore the effect of screen time, cyberbullying, and the impact of web-based entertainment on their youngsters' turn of events.

Balance between serious and fun activities: The requests of present day work and way of life can make it trying for guardians to adjust work and day to day life. This effects how much time and consideration guardians can commit to their kids.

Financial Tensions: Financial tensions can influence the assets accessible to guardians for youngster raising. Monetary differences can prompt inconsistent open doors for youngsters' development and improvement.

Changing Family Designs: Advancing family structures, including single-parent families, mixed families, and same-sex parent families, require transformations in nurturing systems to address the issues of different relational peculiarities.

Chapter 7

Group Dynamics: From Solitary to Social Animals

Collective vibes allude to the investigation of how people interface inside gatherings and how these connections impact the general way of behaving, attachment, and working of the gathering. Perceptions of collective vibes can be made across different species, from single animals to exceptionally friendly creatures, and people. This investigation digs into the assorted scope of overall vibes tracked down in the animals of the world collectively, analyzing the elements that drive social ways of behaving, the advantages of gathering living, and the ramifications of these elements for grasping human social collaborations.

1. **Lone Creatures**
   Qualities of Singular Creatures
   Lone creatures, as the name proposes, are people that essentially live alone and don't take part in bunch ways of behaving. They display explicit attributes that recognize them from social creatures:
   Territoriality: Singular creatures will generally be regional, shielding a particular region or asset against interlopers. This regional way of behaving guarantees admittance to food, mates, and haven.
   Autonomy: Single creatures are to a great extent confident and don't depend on others for hunting, security, or social collaboration.
   Generation: Proliferation in lone creatures is normally a singular exertion. They don't frame stable pair bonds or participate in helpful reproducing.
   Instances of Lone Creatures
   A few animal categories are known for their singular nature, including:
   Tigers: Tigers are lone creatures, with grown-up people keeping up with enormous domains and just meeting up for mating.
   Panthers: Panthers are lone felines that likewise lay out and guard their domains.

Komodo Winged serpents: These enormous reptiles are commonly lone, meeting up just for forceful associations or mating.

2. **Social Creatures**

Qualities of Social Creatures

Social creatures, interestingly, structure and keep up with gatherings, showing a scope of social ways of behaving and qualities:

Participation: Social creatures participate in agreeable exercises, like hunting, guard, and raising posterity. They depend on bunch individuals for different parts of their lives.

Correspondence: Social creatures frequently have complex correspondence frameworks to facilitate bunch exercises, lay out progressive systems, and keep up with social bonds.

Proliferation: In friendly creatures, propagation is in many cases a collective endeavor, with people by and large raising posterity.

Advantages of Sociality

There are a few advantages to living in gatherings, which add to the development of social ways of behaving:

Hunter Guard: Gathering living gives better security against hunters. In a gathering, there are more people to distinguish, deflect, and shield against expected dangers.

Agreeable Hunting: Numerous social creatures take part in helpful hunting, which builds their hunting effectiveness and achievement rates.

Asset Sharing: Living in bunches considers the sharing of assets, like food and safe house. This can be particularly worthwhile in conditions with restricted assets.

Regenerative Advantages: Social creatures can profit from bunch nurturing, as various people can share the obligations of raising posterity. Also, living in gatherings can work with mate determination and mating open doors.

Instances of Social Creatures

There is a wide assortment of social creatures in the collective of animals, including:

Lions: Lions are known for their social way of behaving, living in prides comprising of numerous lionesses and their posterity, with a couple of grown-up guys.

Elephants: Elephants live in very close family bunches drove by authorities. These gatherings take part in helpful childcare and assurance.

Bumble bees: Bumble bee settlements are profoundly organized and social. They take part in complex division of work, with working drones, drones, and a sovereign.

3. **Human Collective vibes**

Advancement of Sociality in People

Sociality plays had a vital impact in human development. Early people framed gatherings for security, asset sharing, and agreeable hunting. Over the long run, human gatherings advanced in intricacy, prompting the improvement of mind boggling social orders and societies.

Attributes of Human Overall vibes

Human collective vibes show one of a kind qualities and intricacies, including:

Correspondence: People have fostered a complex arrangement of language and correspondence, taking into consideration the trading of data, thoughts, and social information inside gatherings.

Social Standards: Human gatherings are administered by social standards, values, and decides that impact conduct, connections, and collaborations inside society.

Social Progressive systems: Human gatherings frequently display social pecking orders, with people possessing different jobs and situations with the gathering.

Participation and Cooperation: People participate in a great many cooperative exercises, from building framework and innovation to chasing after logical and creative undertakings.

Difficulties and Intricacies in Human Collective vibes

Human collective vibes accompany a bunch of difficulties and intricacies, including:

Struggle: Clashes can emerge inside and between gatherings, prompting different types of hostility, rivalry, and questions.

Social Orders: Social progressive systems can prompt disparities and power awkward nature, which can bring about friendly treacheries and separation.

Variety: Human social orders are much of the time described by social, ethnic, and strict variety, which can prompt both participation and struggle.

Variation: People should constantly adjust to evolving social, mechanical, and natural circumstances to keep up with the soundness and prosperity of their gatherings and social orders.

4. **Cross-Species Viewpoints**

Similitudes and Contrasts in Overall vibes

By contrasting collective vibes across species, we can distinguish the two likenesses and contrasts in friendly ways of behaving. Central issues of correlation include:

Collaboration: Participation is a consistent idea in both human and creature overall vibes, driven by the requirement for security, asset sharing, and aggregate activity.

Correspondence: The capacity to impart is vital in both human and creature gatherings. While the intricacy of correspondence shifts, the capability continues as before: to arrange and keep up with bunch attachment.

Social Designs: The two people and a few creatures display social progressive systems, with people possessing explicit jobs and situations with the gathering.

Asset Sharing: The sharing of assets, like food, is seen in both human and creature gatherings. The instruments and social standards for sharing might vary, yet the guideline stays steady.

Suggestions for Human Culture

Understanding collective vibes in the animals of the world collectively gives important experiences to human culture:

Conduct Sciences: Near investigations of collective vibes add to the areas of brain research, human sciences, and social science, revealing insight into the development and working of human social orders.

Natural Effect: Examples from the animals of the world collectively can illuminate conversations about asset sharing, collaboration, and economical living inside human social orders, particularly despite ecological difficulties.

Civil rights: The investigation of collective vibes in the two people and creatures features the significance of tending to social pecking orders, imbalances, and clashes to make all the more and evenhanded social orders.

7.1 The Spectrum of Social Behavior

Social way of behaving is a mind boggling and multi-layered part of human life. It incorporates a great many communications, from cozy one-on-one connections to enormous scope cultural cooperations. The range of social way of behaving is a continuum that incorporates the full scope of human collaborations, from the exceptionally individualistic to the profoundly public. Understanding this range is fundamental for fathoming human instinct and the elements that shape our general public. In this exposition, we will investigate the different elements of the range of social way of behaving, from the individualistic to the public, and analyze how these ways of behaving manifest in various settings.

Individualistic Way of behaving

Toward one side of the range of social way of behaving, we find individualistic way of behaving, which accentuates confidence, individual accomplishment, and freedom. Individualistic way of behaving is frequently connected with societies that esteem individual privileges, opportunity, and individual achievement. In such social orders, individuals are urged to seek after their objectives, express their novel personalities, and pursue free choices.

Individualistic way of behaving is manifest in different ways. It incorporates the quest for individual objectives and desires, the development of one's abilities and interests, and the activity of individual independence. People who display individualistic way of behaving will generally focus on their own requirements and wants over bunch or cultural interests. They are driven by private inspirations and frequently try to stick out or succeed in their picked interests.

In an individualistic culture, contest and accomplishment are exceptionally esteemed. Individuals are urged to go after restricted assets, whether they be instructive open doors, professional successes, or material abundance. The accentuation on contest can prompt areas of strength for an ethic, development, and business, as people endeavor to beat their friends.

In any case, the intense spotlight on independence can likewise have its drawbacks. It might prompt social disconnection, childishness, and an absence of social union. When taken to a limit, independence can disintegrate the feeling of local area and shared liability, possibly adding to social issues like imbalance and the disregard of aggregate requirements.

Common Way of behaving

On the opposite finish of the range, we find common way of behaving, which focuses on the government assistance of the gathering over individual interests. Mutual way of behaving is frequently connected with collectivist societies and social orders where individuals feel areas of strength for an of interconnectedness and shared personality. In such settings, people are urged to coordinate, team up, and cooperate for a long term benefit.

Public way of behaving is obvious in different parts of life, remembering the accentuation for aggregate direction, bunch amicability, and everyone's benefit. Individuals who show public way of behaving are much of the time driven by a feeling of obligation, obligation, and steadfastness to their local area or gathering. They are bound to adjust to laid out standards and customs and may stifle their singular longings for bunch attachment.

In shared social orders, the government assistance of the local area overshadows individual addition. This can prompt areas of strength for an of social help and fortitude. At the point when people share assets and participate, it can bring about a more impartial circulation of riches and valuable open doors, as well as a more noteworthy accentuation on friendly government assistance and security nets.

Nonetheless, the intense spotlight on collective way of behaving can likewise have its disadvantages. It might smother individual innovativeness, drive, and individual articulation. Mindless obedience and similarity can become predominant, possibly ruining advancement and progress. At times, the accentuation on the gathering might prompt the concealment of individual privileges and opportunities.

The Continuum of Social Way of behaving

While individualistic and common ways of behaving address the two limits of the range, most social orders and people fall some in the middle between. The continuum of social way of behaving considers a nuanced comprehension of the different manners by which individuals interface and draw in with their social surroundings.

Adjusting Individual and Common Way of behaving

Finding a harmony among individualistic and common way of behaving is in many cases fundamental for the working of a sound society. Practically speaking, not many social orders or people stick rigorously to one finish of the range. All things considered, a great many people explore a perplexing snare of social connections that expect them to adjust to various settings.

For instance, in the work environment, people frequently need to show individualistic way of behaving to accomplish individual objectives and succeed in their professions. Nonetheless, they additionally need to team up with partners and add to the progress of their association, which requires common way of behaving. Finding some kind of harmony can prompt useful and agreeable workplaces.

Also, in everyday life, people should adjust their own necessities and wants with the prosperity of the nuclear family. Guardians, for example, may focus on their kids' government assistance and satisfaction over their singular desires. In this specific situation, common way of behaving is pivotal for keeping up with family attachment and supporting the future.

Social and Relevant Varieties

The predominance of individualistic or common way of behaving can change altogether across societies and settings. For instance, Western social orders, like the US, frequently underscore independence and individual independence, while Eastern societies, similar to Japan, will quite often focus on shared agreement and gathering attachment.

These social distinctions are formed by verifiable, social, and financial variables, and they impact different parts of life, including relational peculiarities, training, and the work environment. Understanding these social varieties is pivotal for advancing culturally diverse comprehension and powerful correspondence.

Besides, the setting in which people end up can likewise impact their way of behaving. In an emergency or crisis circumstance, individuals may briefly move towards more common way of behaving, helping out others to address the prompt danger. Then again, in the midst of overflow and solidness, they might incline more towards individualistic way of behaving as they seek after private objectives and desires.

Influences on Society

The harmony among individualistic and shared conduct can have significant ramifications for society. A general public that inclines intensely towards independence might encounter more noteworthy financial development and individual flexibility however may likewise wrestle with issues of disparity, social segregation, and an absence of social wellbeing nets.

On the other hand, a general public that inclines emphatically towards shared conduct might succeed in friendly union, impartial asset dissemination, and a solid feeling of local area, yet it might battle with development and individual freedom.

It is fundamental to perceive that the ideal harmony between these two finishes of the range can shift starting with one society then onto the next, and there is nobody size-fits-all methodology. Accomplishing the right equilibrium includes cautious thought of a general public's exceptional history, values, and needs.

The Range of Social Conduct in Present day culture

In contemporary society, the range of social way of behaving is continually developing. Mechanical headways, globalization, and changing accepted practices have reshaped the manner in which individuals collaborate and communicate their thoughts. These progressions have affected the harmony among individualistic and shared conduct.

Innovation and Independence

The ascent of innovation, especially the web and virtual entertainment, has given people exceptional apparatuses for self-articulation and self-advancement. In the computerized age, individual marking, business venture, and the quest for specialty interests have become more open and broad. This has added to the support of individualistic way of behaving, as individuals look to cut out their exceptional computerized personalities.

Nonetheless, the advanced scene isn't without its difficulties. Virtual entertainment stages can likewise encourage selfishness, cyberbullying, and online protected, closed off environments that hinder sound discussion and trade of thoughts. The steady strain to introduce a glorified variant of one's life can add to deep-seated insecurities and social disengagement.

Globalization and Communalism

Globalization has brought individuals from different societies and foundations closer together, setting out open doors for diverse trade and collaboration. As people and social orders become more interconnected, there is a rising consciousness of the requirement for mutual way of behaving to address worldwide difficulties, for example, environmental change, disparity, and general wellbeing.

Public way of behaving is exemplified in worldwide coordinated efforts, helpful endeavors, and aggregate drives to resolve squeezing worldwide issues. While globalization can possibly encourage more noteworthy solidarity and collaboration, it additionally features the abberations in collective qualities and ways of behaving between various countries and districts.

Difficulties and Open doors

As we explore the perplexing range of social conduct in the cutting edge world, there are various moves and potential chances to consider. One of the primary difficulties is finding a harmony among independence and communalism that advances individual prosperity and cultural concordance.

To accomplish this equilibrium, it is crucial for encourage sympathy and understanding among people and networks, perceive the qualities and restrictions of both individualistic and shared conduct, and adjust to changing conditions and social settings.

Training assumes an essential part in shaping the way of behaving of people and social orders. Schools and organizations have an obligation to show values like collaboration, sympathy, and regard for individual freedoms. Moreover, they can give open doors to understudies to participate in cooperative activities and local area administration, advancing both individual development and shared prosperity.

In addition, public strategies and social frameworks should be planned with a view toward striking a decent methodology. This incorporates establishing conditions that boost individual drive and individual accomplishment while additionally giving security nets and systems to social participation. Powerful administration ought to resolve issues like abundance disparity, civil rights, and ecological maintainability.

7.2 Lorenz's Work on Social Structure

Konrad Lorenz, an Austrian zoologist, ethologist, and Nobel laureate, made critical commitments to the investigation of creature conduct and social construction. His work established the groundwork for how we might interpret how creatures, including people, coordinate themselves into gatherings and how these designs impact conduct. Lorenz's work significantly affects the area of ethology, the investigation of creature conduct, and has additionally educated our comprehension regarding human social designs. In this paper, we will investigate Lorenz's critical thoughts and commitments to the investigation of social construction, as well as their ramifications for grasping human social orders.

Ethology and Lorenz's Initial Exploration

Lorenz was a trailblazer in the area of ethology, which looks to grasp the way of behaving of creatures in their common habitats. His work stressed the significance of noticing creatures in their regular territories to acquire experiences into their way of behaving, including social associations. Lorenz's initial examination centered around different species, yet he is maybe most popular for his work with birds, especially geese and ducks.

One of Lorenz's most critical commitments was his perception of engraving, a type of fast learning wherein youthful creatures, typically birds, serious areas of strength for structure to the principal moving item they see, frequently their parent.

This connection is critical for social holding, and it can lastingly affect a creature's social design and conduct. Lorenz's examinations on engraving featured the job of early encounters in forming social connections and connections in creatures.

Ethological Ideas and Social Construction

Lorenz presented a few ideas that have been instrumental in grasping social construction in creature social orders:

1. **Fixed Activity Examples (FAPs):** Lorenz proposed the idea of fixed activity designs, which are cliché ways of behaving set off by unambiguous boosts. FAPs are intrinsic and frequently serve significant social capabilities. For instance, in geese, the FAP of following the mother figure is basic for keeping up with bunch union and learning normal practices.
2. **Intrinsic Delivering Components (IRMs):** These are brain instruments that answer explicit improvements, setting off FAPs. IRMs assume a significant part

in the improvement of social way of behaving. With regards to social construction, IRMs work with the development and upkeep of social bonds by planning activities and reactions inside a gathering.

3. **Ritualization:** Lorenz likewise presented the idea of ritualization, which includes the development of explicit ways of behaving that act as friendly signals and advance coordination inside a gathering. Ritualized ways of behaving help lay out and keep up with social orders, diminish hostility, and improve collaboration among bunch individuals.

Lorenz's Commitments to How we might interpret Human Social Construction

While Lorenz's work fundamentally centered around creature conduct, his bits of knowledge have impacted the investigation of human social construction. The following are a couple of manners by which his thoughts have been applied to human social orders:

1. **Connection Hypothesis:** Lorenz's examination on engraving and connection in creatures laid the foundation for connection hypothesis in brain science. This hypothesis, created by John Bowlby, accentuates the significance of early connection encounters in forming human social connections. It fundamentally affects how we might interpret youngster improvement and grown-up relational connections.

2. **Social Learning and Impersonation:** Lorenz's perceptions on how creatures gain from their current circumstance and copy the way of behaving of others have been reached out to the investigation of human social learning. Social learning hypothesis sets that people secure social ways of behaving, standards, and social practices through perception and impersonation of others, molding the social construction of human social orders.

3. **Ceremonies and Accepted practices:** Lorenz's idea of ritualization and the significance of natural delivering systems in creature social design have been applied to the investigation of human customs, customs, and accepted practices. Ritualized ways of behaving and representative activities assume a significant part in keeping up with social union and sending social qualities in human social orders.

Lorenz's Questionable Thoughts

It is essential to recognize that Lorenz's work has not been without discussion. His thoughts regarding natural animosity in people and the impact of hereditary qualities on conduct have been condemned for their capability to be abused and for misrepresenting complex social peculiarities. Specifically, Lorenz's book "On Animosity" produced huge discussion, as he recommended that people have natural forceful propensities established in their developmental history.

These questionable thoughts, in any case, shouldn't eclipse Lorenz's huge commitments to the area of ethology and our comprehension of social design. While his perspectives on hostility have been tested and reconsidered over the long haul, his work on engraving, connection, and social conduct remains basic in both the investigation of creatures and the comprehension of human social designs.

Lorenz's Impact on Preservation and Natural Morals

Past his commitments to the investigation of creature conduct and social construction, Lorenz was a vocal supporter for preservation and moral treatment of creatures. He stressed the significance of saving regular territories and shielding natural life from human-incited hurt. His thoughts on the moral treatment of creatures and the preservation of biodiversity lastingly affect natural morals and protection endeavors around the world.

7.3 The Role of Dominance and Hierarchy

Strength and pecking order are central parts of social construction and association in different creature species, including people. These ideas assume a basic part in molding social elements, direction, and asset dissemination inside gatherings. Understanding the job of strength and progressive system is vital for appreciating the intricacies of social conduct in both creature and human social orders.

In this article, we will investigate the meaning of strength and order, their developmental beginnings, and their suggestions for human social orders.

1. The Advancement of Strength and Ordered progression

Predominance and progressive system have profound developmental roots that can be followed back to the early progenitors of people and other social creatures. These various leveled frameworks have advanced as versatile systems to address basic endurance and conceptive difficulties. Here are a few central issues on the development of strength and order:

1. **Asset Allotment:** In numerous creature species, admittance to fundamental assets like food, asylum, and mates is much of the time restricted. Pecking orders arise as a method for distributing these assets proficiently. Predominant people frequently have special admittance to these assets, which upgrades their endurance and regenerative achievement.

2. **Diminishing Struggle:** Ordered progressions assist with limiting contentions over assets. At the point when people perceive the power of higher-positioning gathering individuals, it decreases the requirement for consistent forceful contest and lays out request inside the gathering. This is especially invaluable when assets are restricted.

3. **Conceptive Advantages:** Predominant people habitually acquire chances to duplicate and pass on their qualities. In certain species, prevailing guys or females have need admittance to mating accomplices, which can bring about a larger number of posterity.

4. **Social Collaboration:** Progressive system advances social participation by working with the division of work. In numerous creature social orders, people play explicit parts and obligations in light of their position inside the progressive system. This specialization can prompt more proficient gathering working and asset usage.

II. Predominance and Order in Creature Social orders

Pecking orders are pervasive in various creature species, and their designs and elements can differ fundamentally. The following are a couple of instances of how strength and progressive system manifest in various creatures:

1. **Wolves:** Wolf packs are many times described by a reasonable pecking order. The extremely confident man and alpha female stand out and have need admittance to assets and multiplication. Subordinate pack individuals are by and large respectful and help with hunting and raising the alpha pair's posterity.

2. **Primates:** Many primates, like chimpanzees and monkeys, have obvious pecking orders. Strength frequently includes actual animosity, however it can likewise be laid out through friendly coalitions and prepping. High-positioning people appreciate special admittance to food and mates.

3. **Birds:** Avian species, including chickens and flying predators, display pecking orders inside their groups. Predominance can be laid out through showcases of hostility or strength customs. High-positioning birds frequently approach the best settling destinations and better food sources.

III. Predominance and Order in Human Social orders

In human social orders, predominance and progressive system additionally assume pivotal parts in forming social designs and collaborations. While human pecking orders are many times more perplexing and multi-layered than those in creature social orders, they share a few normal highlights:

1. **Economic wellbeing:** Human social orders have an idea of societal position that is frequently connected with riches, influence, or esteem. Economic wellbeing is an essential determinant of a singular's situation in the social pecking order.

2. **Progressive Associations:** Pecking orders are available in different human foundations and associations, including government, military, organizations, and schooling. These pecking orders are organized with plainly characterized jobs and authority levels.

3. **Imbalance:** Human social orders show changing levels of social and financial disparity, which are in many cases reflected in progressive designs. Those with higher economic wellbeing might appreciate better admittance to assets, training, and medical services.

4. **Social Variety:** The idea of human orders can fluctuate across societies. Various social orders put various qualities on properties like age, orientation, and abundance while deciding a singular's societal position.

IV. The Effect of Strength and Ordered progression on Human Social orders

The job of strength and ordered progression in human social orders has expansive ramifications for social way of behaving, collaboration, and struggle. Here are a portion of the key effects:

1. **Imbalance:** Ordered progressions can sustain social and monetary disparity. Those at the top frequently have more critical admittance to assets and amazing open doors, while those at the base might confront hindrances to social portability.

2. **Inspiration and Desire:** The craving to climb the social order can act as serious areas of strength for a for people. Many individuals seek to accomplish higher status, which can drive development, contest, and individual accomplishment.

3. **Solidness:** Orders can add to social soundness by giving a reasonable design to independent direction and authority. This can be advantageous in the midst of emergency or when fast reactions are required.

4. **Struggle and Discontent:** Orders can likewise prompt clash and social turmoil. At the point when individuals see the framework as low or shifty, it can bring about fights, developments, or even upsets.

5. **Orientation Jobs:** Orientation based progressive systems have generally been predominant in numerous social orders, molding assumptions and jobs for people. Contemporary endeavors mean to move and change these orders to accomplish orientation equity.

V. The Difficult exercise: Finding Some kind of harmony in Human Social orders

While progressive systems can serve significant capabilities in human social orders, it is essential to find some kind of harmony between keeping social control and resolving issues of disparity and unfairness. Here are a few contemplations for accomplishing this equilibrium:

1. **Meritocracy:** Empowering meritocracy, where people are compensated in light of their capacities and endeavors as opposed to their acquired status, can assist with decreasing social imbalance and advance reasonableness.

2. **Social Wellbeing Nets:** Carrying out friendly security nets, like admittance to medical services, instruction, and essential pay, can assist with relieving the adverse consequences of imbalance and give open doors to those at the lower rungs of the progressive system.

3. **Social Portability:** Encouraging social versatility, where people have the valuable chance to climb the progressive system in view of their accomplishments, can make pecking orders more unique and receptive to individual exertion.

4. **Inclusivity:** Advancing inclusivity and variety in different social foundations can challenge customary pecking orders in view of orientation, race, and different elements.

5. **Moral Authority:** Pioneers in various leveled associations and organizations ought to stick to moral standards and focus on the prosperity of those they lead, as opposed to keeping up with their own power and honor.

7.4Lessons for Understanding Human Communities

Human people group, whether they are little areas, enormous urban communities, or worldwide social orders, are mind boggling and dynamic elements. Understanding them requires a multidisciplinary approach that consolidates bits of knowledge from humanism, humanities, brain research, financial matters, and different fields. In this article, we will investigate a few key examples that offer important experiences into fathoming human networks and the variables that shape them. These illustrations envelop different perspectives, from the significance of culture and informal communities to the job of force and imbalance in forming networks.

Culture is the Foundation of Networks

Culture is a primary component in figuring out human networks. Culture includes shared convictions, values, standards, customs, and customs that tight spot people together inside a local area. These social components assume a focal part in molding local area character and characterizing how individuals connect with each other.

Social variety inside and among networks is a demonstration of the rich embroidery of human social orders. Understanding and regarding these social distinctions is fundamental for encouraging collaboration and agreeable concurrence among assorted networks. Social capability and culturally diverse relational abilities are significant apparatuses for crossing over holes and building more grounded associations between networks.

Informal organizations Are the Structure Blocks of Networks

Human people group are geological or hierarchical substances as well as are unpredictably associated through informal communities. Informal communities are the trap of connections that interface people, families, gatherings, and associations inside a local area. These organizations are fundamental for the progression of data, assets, and social help.

The construction and elements of informal organizations impact the union and working of networks. Concentrating on these organizations can assist us with understanding how data and ways of behaving spread, how accepted practices are laid out, and how friendly capital is constructed. The advanced age has extended the extent of informal organizations, giving new experiences into virtual networks and online associations.

Power Elements Shape People group

Power elements are a central part of local area life. Networks frequently have pioneers, specialists, or power structures that impact navigation, asset circulation, and normal practices. Perceiving and breaking down these power elements is essential for understanding how networks capability and resolving issues of imbalance and civil rights.

The conveyance of force inside networks can prompt either comprehensive or selective conditions. Comprehensive people group enable all individuals to partake in navigation and asset distribution, cultivating a feeling of having a place and value. Elite people group concentrate power among a chosen handful, prompting social variations and divisions.

Imbalance and Its Effect on Networks

Imbalance is an unavoidable issue that influences networks at nearby, public, and worldwide levels. Financial, social, and political abberations can sabotage local area union and prosperity. Understanding the drivers and outcomes of disparity is fundamental for making more comprehensive and strong networks.

Imbalances in pay, admittance to schooling, medical care, and lodging can fuel social divisions and frustrate aggregate advancement. It is basic to address these disparities through approaches, projects, and drives that advance equivalent open doors and civil rights. Feasible turn of events and neediness decrease endeavors are key to building more evenhanded networks.

Local area Versatility and Transformation

Networks face a scope of difficulties, from cataclysmic events and monetary slumps to social emergencies and general wellbeing crises. The limit of a local area to endure and recuperate from these difficulties is a proportion of its strength. Building versatile networks includes cultivating participation, readiness, and flexibility.

Understanding how networks adjust to change and assemble versatility can illuminate procedures for tending to future difficulties. Local area based calamity readiness, ecological protection, and social security nets are instances of drives that upgrade local area strength.

The Job of Normal practices and Organizations

Normal practices and establishments assume a basic part in deeply shaping human way of behaving and local area elements. Standards are unwritten principles and assumptions that guide human cooperations, while establishments are formal associations and frameworks that structure cultural capabilities.

The impact of normal practices should be visible in different parts of local area life, from family designs and orientation jobs to moral qualities and social practices. Establishments, like legislatures, schooling systems, and lawful structures, give the framework to local area administration and social request.

The Effect of Urbanization

The quick development of urban areas and metropolitan regions has changed the idea of human networks. Urbanization presents the two open doors and difficulties for understanding and overseeing networks. Metropolitan regions are center points of financial action, social trade, and advancement, yet they additionally face issues connected with blockage, natural maintainability, and social abberations.

The investigation of metropolitan networks gives experiences into the elements of relocation, variety, and metropolitan preparation. The production of reasonable, comprehensive, and feasible urban areas is a focal objective for tending to the intricacies of metropolitan networks.

Networks in a Globalized World

The course of globalization has achieved interconnectedness between networks on a worldwide scale. Monetary, political, and social trades happen across borders, affecting networks in different ways. Understanding the ramifications of globalization on networks is fundamental for resolving transnational issues and building a more interconnected world.

Worldwide difficulties, for example, environmental change, pandemics, and movement, require cooperative endeavors and worldwide administration. Networks are not generally restricted to neighborhood or public limits however are progressively impacted by global powers.

Networks and Innovation

Headways in innovation have reformed the manner in which networks capability and collaborate. The ascent of the web, virtual entertainment, and advanced stages has reshaped correspondence, data sharing, and social association. Innovation can possibly associate individuals across geographic distances and impact local area elements.

Understanding the job of innovation in networks includes looking at its effect on friendly connections, admittance to data, and the arrangement of virtual networks. Issues connected with computerized separation, security, and network safety are basic to the investigation of networks in the advanced age.

The Human Component in Local area Getting it

Ultimately, perceiving the meaning of the human component in understanding communities is fundamental. Networks are made out of people with different encounters, points of view, and desires. Human organization, joint effort, and aggregate activity are vital to the turn of events and prosperity of networks.

Specialists, policymakers, and local area pioneers should include local area individuals during the time spent understanding and working on their networks. Enabling people to effectively partake in local area direction and improvement endeavors is essential for making stronger, comprehensive, and flourishing networks.

Chapter 8

King Solomon's Ring: The Eponymous Discovery

The legend of Ruler Solomon's Ring has caught human creative mind for quite a long time. Established in old fables and strict customs, this amazing antique is related with the scriptural Ruler Solomon, known for his insight, abundance, and momentous rule. The narrative of Lord Solomon's Ring is a captivating story that consolidates components of history, religion, and folklore. It has been a wellspring of motivation for writing, craftsmanship, and philosophical conversations. In this article, we will investigate the starting points and different understandings of the legend of Ruler Solomon's Ring, revealing insight into its importance and persevering through impact.

Lord Solomon: The Shrewd and Well off Ruler

Prior to diving into the narrative of Ruler Solomon's Ring, understanding the verifiable and scriptural setting of Lord Solomon himself is fundamental. Solomon, the child of Ruler David and Bathsheba, is a noticeable figure in the Jewish Book of scriptures, known for his insight and riches. He ruled over the Unified Realm of Israel and is customarily accepted to have managed around 970-931 BCE. During his rule, he is said to have changed Israel into a prosperous and persuasive realm.

Ruler Solomon is generally prestigious for his amazing insight, which is portrayed in the scriptural story of the two ladies who professed to be the mother of a similar child. Solomon's wise judgment in proposing to isolate the child to save its life procured him the standing of being a shrewd and fair ruler. His insight was additionally exhibited through his compositions, especially the Book of Axioms and the Tune of Solomon.

Furthermore, Solomon's riches and wonder are generally celebrated in both authentic records and scriptural texts. His wealth were represented by the renowned "Solomon's Sanctuary," which was built in Jerusalem. The sanctuary was decorated with valuable materials, including gold, silver, and cedar wood, underlining the realm's extravagance.

The Beginnings of the Legend

The tale of Lord Solomon's Ring, while not straightforwardly tracked down in the scriptural texts, is established in Jewish fables and later spread to different societies and strict practices.

The ring, accepted to have supernatural abilities, turned into an image of Solomon's insight, command over nature, and his capacity to speak with creatures.

One of the earliest Jewish texts where the account of Lord Solomon's Ring is referenced is "The Confirmation of Solomon," a fanciful text dated between the first and third hundreds of years CE. In this text, Solomon is an otherworldly portrayed as a ruler ring to control and order evil presences to help in the development of the Primary Sanctuary. This ring was engraved with a pentagram, an image generally connected with Solomon, alongside the name of God and a mystery expression, which permitted him to control and speak with spirits.

The account acquired further noticeable quality in archaic Jewish, Christian, and Islamic texts, tales, and legends. It is crucial for note that varieties of the story exist in various societies, with varying translations and traits allocated to the ring.

Translations of Ruler Solomon's Ring

Lord Solomon's Ring has been deciphered in different ways, contingent upon social, strict, and scholarly viewpoints. Here are a portion of the essential translations:

Intelligence and Information: Lord Solomon's Ring represents his excellent insight and information. In the fanciful stories, the ring gives him the ability to figure out the dialects of creatures, permitting him to speak with them and gain understanding into their regular ways of behaving. This translation highlights that shrewdness is a vital aspect for understanding and orchestrating with the regular world.

Command over Nature: In certain translations, the ring awards Solomon command over the powers of nature. This power is exemplified by his capacity to order the spirits and creatures, as well as by the legends of his dominance over the breeze and water. Such control represents the dominance of human mind over the regular world.

Divine Power: Lord Solomon's Ring is much of the time considered an indication of heavenly power. It connotes his exceptional relationship with God, who allowed him the capacity to speak with creatures and other heavenly creatures. It highlights his heavenly arrangement as a ruler and his job in building the Principal Sanctuary in Jerusalem.

Moral Examples: The account of Lord Solomon's Ring additionally conveys moral illustrations. In certain translations, it fills in as an update that shrewdness ought to be utilized for kindhearted purposes and that power should be practiced mindfully. Solomon's insight is viewed as an excellence, and his utilization of the ring is a demonstration of the significance of moral direct.

Fables and Legend: In folkloric customs, the legend of Lord Solomon's Ring is embraced as a dazzling and creative story. The idea of a mysterious ring that permits correspondence with creatures and the control of powerful elements holds an inherent allure and has been sustained through narrating.

Philosophical and Scholarly Motivation: The legend of Lord Solomon's Ring has likewise been a wellspring of motivation for savants, journalists, and craftsmen. It has been integrated into different works of writing, for example, the "Solomonic" writing of the Medieval times, and has filled in as a topical component in various philosophical conversations about shrewdness, power, and the human instinct relationship.

Impact on Craftsmanship and Culture

The account of Ruler Solomon's Ring has made a permanent imprint on workmanship, culture, and writing. Its impact should be visible in different types of imaginative articulation, from writing to works of art, music, and movies. Here are a few remarkable instances of its impact:

Writing: Ruler Solomon's Ring has been a repetitive theme in writing. Striking works, like Gustave Flaubert's "The Allurement of Holy person Anthony" and Gabriel García Márquez's "100 Years of Isolation," reference the ring in their accounts. These references frequently convey representative importance connected with insight and power.

Visual Expressions: Artworks and outlines including Lord Solomon's Ring have been made by various specialists throughout the long term. These works of art commonly portray Solomon with the mystical ring in different scenes, underscoring his insight and association with creatures.

Music: The tale of Lord Solomon's Ring has propelled melodic pieces. For instance, the German writer Carl Orff made a show named "Der Mond" (The Moon), which incorporates a scene highlighting the popular judgment of Ruler Solomon and the presence of his unbelievable ring.

Film and TV: Components of the story have advanced into movies and network shows. Whether unequivocally or as a metaphorical reference, the possibility of a strong, mysterious ring that conveys shrewdness and control is a repetitive subject in dream and experience stories.

Imagery: Ruler Solomon's Ring is likewise utilized as an image in different settings. It might address the force of insight, the connection among mankind and the normal world, or the association between the natural and the heavenly domains. The ring is frequently used to pass on messages about the overall influence and obligation.

8.1 The Story Behind the Ring

The legend of Ruler Solomon's Ring, an image of intelligence, power, and magical correspondence with the normal world, has entranced and fascinated individuals for a really long time. Established in strict texts, fables, and old customs, the tale of the ring exemplifies a mix of history and legend that keeps on charming the human creative mind. In this exposition, we will dive into the beginnings, verifiable setting, and understandings of the legend of Lord Solomon's Ring, investigating the getting through charm and the different features of this fascinating story.

Lord Solomon and His Unprecedented Insight

Prior to diving into the tale of Ruler Solomon's Ring, understanding the authentic and scriptural setting of Lord Solomon is fundamental. Solomon, the child of Lord David and Bathsheba, is an unmistakable figure in the Jewish Book of scriptures, known for his exceptional insight and rich rule. He is generally accepted to have ruled over the Assembled Realm of Israel around 970-931 BCE. During his standard, he changed Israel into a prosperous and compelling realm.

Lord Solomon's amazing insight is among his most prestigious characteristics. His standing as a shrewd and fair ruler is best shown in the renowned scriptural story of the two ladies who professed to be the mother of a similar child. Solomon's proposition to partition the child to save its life and distinguish the genuine mother exhibited his striking judgment and insight.

Besides, Lord Solomon's insight is apparent through his works, quite the Book of Adages and the Melody of Solomon, the two of which investigate different aspects of human existence, morals, and love. His rule is likewise connected with the development of the Principal Sanctuary in Jerusalem, an image of the realm's magnificence and success.

The Legend of Ruler Solomon's Ring

The tale of Ruler Solomon's Ring, however not straightforwardly tracked down in the scriptural texts, is established in Jewish fables and later spread to different societies and strict practices. The legend portrays Solomon as a ruler with the capacity to speak with creatures and control otherworldly creatures, all because of an enchanted ring.

The earliest recorded notice of the ring can be tracked down in the spurious text "The Confirmation of Solomon," dating between the first and third hundreds of years CE. This text portrays Solomon's utilization of the ring to order and control evil spirits to aid the development of the Principal Sanctuary. The ring is portrayed as having a pentagram, an image frequently connected with Solomon, and engraved with the name of God and a mystery expression, which conceded him domain over these otherworldly creatures.

The account acquired further conspicuousness in archaic Jewish, Christian, and Islamic texts, as well as in classic stories and legends. In any case, it is pivotal to take note of that varieties of the story exist in various societies, each with its own translation and qualities allocated to the ring.

Understandings of Ruler Solomon's Ring

The legend of Ruler Solomon's Ring has been deciphered in different ways, mirroring the social, strict, and scholarly viewpoints of various social orders. Here are a portion of the essential understandings:

Intelligence and Information: Ruler Solomon's Ring is in many cases deciphered as an image of his unprecedented insight and information. As per the legend, the ring allowed him the ability to figure out the dialects of creatures, empowering him to speak with them and gain understanding into their ways of behaving. This translation highlights that intelligence is vital to understanding and blending with the regular world.

Command over Nature: In certain translations, the ring awards Solomon command over the powers of nature. This power is exemplified by his capacity to order spirits and creatures, as well as by legends of his dominance over regular components like breeze and water. Such control represents the possibility that human acumen can have domain over the regular world.

Divine Power: Ruler Solomon's Ring is many times considered to be an indication of heavenly power. It implies his unique relationship with God, who allowed him the capacity to speak with creatures and other extraordinary elements. It highlights his heavenly arrangement as a ruler and his job in building the Primary Sanctuary in Jerusalem.

Moral Illustrations: The account of Ruler Solomon's Ring conveys moral examples in certain understandings. It fills in as an update that shrewdness ought to be utilized for considerate purposes and that power should be practiced capably. Solomon's insight is viewed as a goodness, and his utilization of the ring is a demonstration of the significance of moral lead.

Old stories and Legend: In folkloric customs, the legend of Ruler Solomon's Ring is embraced as an enamoring and creative story. The idea of a mystical ring that permits correspondence with creatures and the control of otherworldly substances holds inborn allure and has been propagated through narrating.

Philosophical and Scholarly Motivation: The legend of Ruler Solomon's Ring has likewise been a wellspring of motivation for rationalists, essayists, and craftsmen. It has been integrated into different works of writing, for example, the "Solomonic" writing of the Medieval times, and has filled in as a topical component in various philosophical conversations about shrewdness, power, and the human instinct relationship.

Impact on Workmanship and Culture

The account of Ruler Solomon's Ring has made a permanent imprint on craftsmanship, culture, and writing. Its impact can be seen in different types of creative articulation, from writing to artworks, music, and movies. Here are a few striking instances of its impact:

Writing: Ruler Solomon's Ring has been a repetitive theme in writing. Eminent works, like Gustave Flaubert's "The Allurement of Holy person Anthony" and Gabriel García Márquez's "100 Years of Isolation," reference the ring in their accounts. These references frequently convey emblematic importance connected with insight and power.

Visual Expressions: Artworks and representations highlighting Lord Solomon's Ring have been made by various specialists throughout the long term. These works of art ordinarily portray Solomon with the otherworldly ring in different scenes, underscoring his insight and association with creatures.

Music: The account of Lord Solomon's Ring has motivated melodic sytheses. For instance, the German writer Carl Orff made a drama named "Der Mond" (The Moon), which incorporates a scene including the well known judgment of Ruler Solomon and the presence of his unbelievable ring.

Film and TV: Components of the story have advanced into movies and TV programs. Whether expressly or as a figurative reference, the possibility of a strong, otherworldly ring that conveys shrewdness and control is a repetitive topic in dream and experience stories.

Imagery: Lord Solomon's Ring is likewise utilized as an image in different settings. It might address the force of intelligence, the connection among mankind and the regular world, or the association between the natural and the heavenly domains. The ring is frequently used to pass on messages about the overall influence and obligation.

8.2 Lorenz's Experiment with Jackdaws

Konrad Lorenz, a spearheading Austrian ethologist, is eminent for his weighty examination on creature conduct and engraving. Among his numerous commitments to the field, one of the most interesting and celebrated tests was his work with jackdaws. In this article, we will investigate Lorenz's examination with jackdaws, the philosophy he utilized, the discoveries he got, and the more extensive ramifications for how we might interpret creature conduct and engraving.

Konrad Lorenz: The Ethologist

Konrad Lorenz (1903-1989) was an unmistakable figure in the area of ethology, the logical investigation of creature conduct. He is frequently alluded to as one of the principal architects of this discipline, alongside other outstanding ethologists like Nikolaas Tinbergen and Karl von Frisch. Lorenz's work significantly affects how we might interpret the way of behaving of different species, particularly birds.

One of Lorenz's most critical commitments to ethology was his idea of engraving. Engraving alludes to the cycle by which certain creatures structure solid, quick, and irreversible connections to explicit items or people during a basic period in their initial turn of events. Lorenz's analyses with jackdaws were instrumental in the improvement of this idea and gave significant experiences into creature conduct.

The Jackdaw: A Friendly Corvid

The jackdaw (Coloeus monedula) is a types of corvid, a gathering of birds known for their insight and complex social ways of behaving. Jackdaws are little, dark plumaged birds with particular dim scruffs and pale eyes. They are exceptionally amiable and frequently tracked down in huge groups. These birds are known for their exceptional critical abilities to think and the development of complicated social orders inside their gatherings.

Lorenz's Analysis with Jackdaws

Lorenz's investigation with jackdaws essentially centered around engraving and the birds' intrinsic acknowledgment and connection to explicit visual boosts. Coming up next is an outline of the investigation's procedure and the key discoveries:

Hatchery Examination: Lorenz led his trial during the 1930s, during the reproducing time of the jackdaws. He gathered eggs from the homes of wild jackdaws and brought forth them in a hatchery. This approach permitted Lorenz to control the early raising climate of the birds and intently notice their turn of events.

Visual Upgrades: In the analysis, Lorenz utilized different visual improvements to evaluate the birds' engraving conduct. He gave the youthful jackdaws a scope of items, including gloves, veils, and other lifeless things. Notwithstanding, the most striking and significant piece of the examination included Lorenz himself.

Human Engraving: Lorenz acquainted the youthful jackdaws with himself during their basic time of engraving. He wore an unmistakable white coat, which incorporated a huge mouth like veil and other prominent elements. Lorenz guaranteed that the jackdaws saw him during the basic time frame, which is normally inside the initial not many hours or days subsequent to incubating.

Connection and Acknowledgment: The significant aftereffect of Lorenz's examination was that the youthful jackdaws engraved on him. They perceived Lorenz, explicitly his hidden appearance, as their parental figure and defender. This connection was areas of strength for strikingly continued all through their lives.

Key Discoveries and Suggestions

Lorenz's investigation with jackdaws yielded a few significant discoveries and experiences into creature conduct and engraving:

Engraving as an Endurance System: Lorenz's investigation gave proof that engraving is a versatile instrument that helps youthful creatures perceive and connect to their guardian, guaranteeing their endurance. In the wild, this guardian is regularly the parent or one more individual from similar species.

Irreversible Nature of Engraving: The examination featured the irreversible idea of engraving. When the jackdaws had engraved on Lorenz, they couldn't shape areas of strength for similar with individuals from their own species or different articles, like gloves or covers. This perpetual quality of engraving is a critical element of the interaction.

Explicitness of Engraving: The investigation exhibited the particularity of engraving. The jackdaws engraved on Lorenz's unmistakable appearance instead of on a more broad human structure. This particularity is steady with different perceptions in the set of all animals, where youthful creatures engrave on unambiguous attributes or boosts.

Family Acknowledgment: Lorenz's work additionally shed light on the significance of family acknowledgment in creature conduct. The jackdaws' connection to Lorenz recommends that they saw him as an individual from their own species or a proxy parent. This part of engraving adds to the improvement of social securities and ways of behaving inside creature networks.

Commitments to Ethology: Lorenz's investigation with jackdaws altogether added to the area of ethology. His work featured the significance of early encounters and the job of engraving in shaping creature conduct. It prepared for additional examination into the systems of engraving in different species.

Past the Jackdaws: The More extensive Ramifications

Lorenz's examination with jackdaws is only one of many examples in which engraving has been seen across species. Engraving assumes a significant part in the improvement of different creature ways of behaving, including:

Parent-Posterity Connection: In numerous species, engraving guarantees areas of strength for an among guardians and their posterity. This connection is fundamental for the arrangement of care, security, and endurance.

Mate Determination: Engraving can likewise impact mate choice, as it directs a singular's inclination for potential accomplices in light of the engraving experience during its initial turn of events.

Species Distinguishing proof: Engraving helps creatures in recognizing individuals from their own species. It is especially significant in the acknowledgment of conspecifics during connections and mating.

Territory Determination: A few animal varieties engrave on their natal living space, which impacts their future decisions in choosing reasonable conditions for scavenging, settling, or reproducing.

Learning and Critical thinking: Engraving might work with the acquiring of explicit abilities or ways of behaving that are pivotal for a creature's endurance, like scavenging strategies or correspondence.

Lorenz's work with jackdaws, while well defined for this specific species, has more extensive ramifications for how we might interpret engraving and its part in shaping creature conduct. The trial showed the way that engraving can happen across a scope of creature animal groups and is a basic cycle in the improvement of social bonds and ways of behaving.

8.3 The Significance of Imprinting

Engraving is a striking and perplexing peculiarity that happens during the early formative phases of numerous creature species. It includes the development of solid and frequently irreversible connections between youthful creatures and explicit articles, people, or improvements. This cycle assumes a vital part in forming different parts of creature conduct, from parent-posterity connection to mate determination and social communications. In this exposition, we will dive into the meaning of engraving, investigating its different structures, the systems behind it, and its more extensive ramifications in the set of all animals.

Characterizing Engraving

Engraving is a type of quick discovering that happens during a basic or delicate period right off the bat in a creature's life. This basic period commonly compares to when the creature is especially open to tactile encounters and upgrades. During this period, youthful creatures are bound to areas of strength for shape enduring connections to explicit items, people, or elements in their current circumstance.

The most notable type of engraving is obedient engraving, which includes the holding of youthful creatures to their folks or guardians. Notwithstanding, engraving can likewise envelop different kinds of connections, including sexual engraving (mate inclination), territory engraving (decision of a particular climate), and, surprisingly, social engraving (ID and holding with conspecifics).

Systems of Engraving

The systems behind engraving are perplexing and not yet completely comprehended. In any case, there are a few key components that assume a part in this peculiarity:

Delicate Period: Engraving happens during a touchy or basic period in a creature's initial turn of events. This period is described by uplifted receptivity to tangible encounters and upgrades. The planning of the basic time frame can fluctuate among species and, surprisingly, inside various people of similar species.

Irreversibility: Engraving is frequently irreversible. When a creature has engraved on a particular item or individual, it is trying to change or fix this connection. The lastingness of engraving is one of its characterizing highlights.

Explicitness: Engraving is explicit. Youthful creatures will quite often engrave on specific qualities or boosts. For instance, ducklings might engrave on the visual and hear-able prompts of their mom's quacking, while different species might engrave on various tactile signals.

Job of Guardians: Parental figures or parental figures regularly assume a focal part in the engraving system, especially in dutiful engraving. Youthful creatures figure out how to perceive and append to their guardians, who give care, assurance, and endurance benefits.

The Meaning of Engraving

Parent-Posterity Connection

One of the main parts of engraving is its job in serious areas of strength for encouraging posterity connections. This connection is basic for the endurance and prosperity of numerous creature species. Engraving guarantees that youthful creatures perceive and bond with their guardians, making them bound to get the vital consideration, assurance, and sustenance during their beginning phases of life.

In species like birds, for example, ducks and geese, obedient engraving guarantees that posterity follow their folks and stay near them. This connection is especially significant for species with precocial youthful, which are brought into the world in a further developed state and are fit for moving soon after birth. These youthful creatures need the direction and insurance of their folks to explore the world and acquire fundamental basic instincts.

Mate Choice

Engraving stretches out past parent-posterity connections and furthermore impacts mate choice in different creature species. Sexual engraving, specifically, is a basic part of mate choice. This cycle includes youthful creatures engraving on specific qualities or attributes, frequently founded on the highlights of their guardians or different conspecifics during the basic time frame.

For instance, numerous types of birds, like larks, figure out how to perceive the tunes and viewable prompts of expected mates during their initial turn of events. This engraving on unambiguous characteristics assumes a critical part in the later determination of reasonable accomplices for propagation. The mates picked are normally those that show highlights like those on which the individual engraved.

Living space Determination

Engraving isn't restricted to social and sexual connections; it additionally impacts territory determination in different species. Living space engraving happens when youthful creatures figure out how to perceive and favor explicit conditions during the basic time frame. This interaction can have significant ramifications for the creatures' future scavenging, reproducing, and endurance.

For instance, salmon engraving on the trail of the waterway or stream where they are conceived. This engraving helps guide them back to their natal waters when it is the ideal opportunity for producing. Such accuracy in natural surroundings determination is imperative for the regenerative achievement and endurance of these fish.

Species ID

Engraving can likewise assume a part in animal categories distinguishing proof, permitting creatures to perceive and bond with individuals from their own species. Youthful creatures might engrave on the visual, hear-able, or olfactory prompts well defined for their species. This acknowledgment is urgent for social associations and mating.

In certain types of penguins, for instance, chicks gain proficiency with the one of a kind vocal calls of their folks during the touchy period. This vocal engraving assists chicks with recognizing their folks in a thickly populated and loud rearing state, guaranteeing that they get legitimate consideration and sustenance.

Learning and Critical thinking

Engraving can work with the mastering of explicit abilities or ways of behaving that are fundamental for a creature's endurance. For instance, in precocial species, youthful creatures might engrave on their folks' searching strategies or route abilities. These learned ways of behaving give an establishment to future free living.

The Importance Past Endurance

While engraving's essential importance lies in the endurance and prosperity of creatures, it likewise has more extensive ramifications for how we might interpret discernment, learning, and the advancement of perplexing ways of behaving. Engraving is a striking illustration of how early encounters and tangible information shape a creature's view of the world and impact its future collaborations and choices.

Additionally, engraving has caught the interest of analysts, teachers, and progressives the same. Understanding the components and meaning of engraving isn't simply major to the areas of ethology and social environment yet additionally has applications in different regions, like untamed life the board, protection endeavors, and creature cultivation.

8.4 Modern Applications and Implications

Engraving, a peculiarity at first found and broadly concentrated on in ethology, has sweeping ramifications and applications in the cutting edge world. Understanding the instruments and meaning of engraving goes past the domain of creature conduct research. It has tracked down applications in different fields, from brain research and neuroscience to preservation and schooling. In this paper, we will investigate the advanced applications and ramifications of engraving, revealing insight into how this idea proceeds to impact and improve how we might interpret human and creature conduct, as well as its viable applications in genuine settings.

Brain research and Neuroscience

Engraving, at first concentrated on with regards to creatures, has educated our comprehension regarding human brain research and neuroscience. While the idea of engraving may not be straightforwardly relevant to people similarly it is to sure creature species, it has roused research in the accompanying regions:

1. **Connection Hypothesis:** The spearheading work of John Bowlby on connection hypothesis was impacted by ethological ideas, including engraving. Connection hypothesis sets that early profound bonds framed among kids and their parental figures assume a significant part in forming human connections and close to home turn of events.

2. **Basic Periods:** The possibility of delicate or basic periods in early turn of events, similar to the basic time frames saw in engraving, has been applied to human formative brain science. Analysts have concentrated on what early encounters and tactile info mean for human mental and profound turn of events.

3. **Brain adaptability:** Engraving has added to how we might interpret brain adaptability — the cerebrum's capacity to adjust and redesign itself in light of encounters. Research in neuroscience has investigated how early tangible encounters and connections can impact mental health and brain associations.

Schooling and Learning

Engraving standards have affected instructive practices and speculations, especially in the field of youth schooling:

1. **Language Obtaining:** Engraving like components have been applied to the investigation of language securing in youngsters. Early openness to language and semantic boosts is thought of as pivotal for language advancement. This idea has informed language drenching programs and early language training.

2. **Mental Turn of events:** The investigation of mental improvement in youngsters has been impacted by the possibility of touchy periods. Understanding how

youngsters get major mental abilities, like number sense and spatial thinking, has suggestions for instructive systems and educational program plan.

Preservation and Creature Conduct

Engraving assumes a significant part in preservation endeavors and the comprehension of creature conduct:

1. **Hostage Rearing Projects:** Traditionalists use engraving standards to work with the renewed introduction of imperiled species into nature. By raising youthful creatures in conditions where they can engrave on conspecific prompts and regular habitats, they improve the probability of effective renewed introduction.
2. **Concentrating on Creature Conduct:** The investigation of engraving has advanced our insight into creature conduct, helping untamed life analysts in figuring out species-explicit ways of behaving and social elements. This data is fundamental for untamed life the board, preservation, and the security of environments.
3. **Creature Cultivation:** Engraving standards have useful applications in creature farming. For example, engraving on people in specific tamed species, like sheep and goats, can work with taking care of, the board, and care rehearses.

Moral and Moral Ramifications

Engraving research and its applications raise moral and moral contemplations:

1. **Creature Government assistance:** Engraving in hostage conditions, for example, zoos and recovery focuses, can bring up moral issues. The most common way of engraving on people, while functional for overseers, may have long haul ramifications for a creature's prosperity and regular way of behaving.
2. **Human Mediation:** The utilization of engraving standards in human mediations, for example, language submersion programs or early training, prompts conversations on the harmony between animating learning and regarding the youngster's formative requirements.

Human-Creature Communications

Engraving research has suggestions for our communications with creatures:

1. **Human-Creature Bond:** Understanding engraving makes sense of areas of strength for the that can shape among people and creatures. It has applications in creature helped treatment, administration creatures, and the consideration of buddy creatures.

2. **Creature Preparing:** Standards of engraving and understanding the basic times of learning can direct viable creature preparing and changing on a surface level. Engraving ideas impact uplifting feedback based preparing techniques.

Innovation and Mechanical technology

Engraving ideas have motivated progressions in innovation and mechanical technology:

1. **Robot Conduct:** Scientists have investigated the use of engraving standards in planning robots with versatile way of behaving. These robots can gain from their current circumstance, adjust to client inclinations, and show more similar collaborations.
2. **Human-Robot Cooperation:** Engraving motivated robots have possible applications in fields like medical services, where mechanical colleagues can adjust to individual patient requirements and give customized care.

Language and Correspondence

The idea of engraving has applications in the investigation of language and correspondence:

1. **Discourse Acknowledgment and Handling:** Understanding what early openness to language means for discourse discernment and language improvement has suggestions for discourse acknowledgment innovation and normal language handling.
2. **Cross-Semantic Exploration:** Engraving roused examination can assist with making sense of the distinctions in language obtaining and articulation among people presented to various dialects during delicate periods.

Social Customs and Practices

In certain societies, certain practices are affected by engraving ideas:

1. **Social Customs:** Social practices connected with youngster raising and early training might be educated by convictions about touchy periods and the significance of early encounters.
2. **Nurturing Styles:** The comprehension of early turn of events and connection has impacted nurturing styles, with an accentuation on establishing secure and supporting conditions for kids.

Human-Creature Half and half Exploration

In logical exploration, especially in hereditary qualities and regenerative medication, engraving standards have significance:

1. **Hereditary Change:** Understanding the epigenetic systems hidden engraving can illuminate hereditary alteration and cloning strategies, including the production of human-creature half and halves for clinical examination.
2. **Regenerative Medication:** Engraving instruments have suggestions for regenerative medication, where researchers concentrate on cell reinventing to create explicit tissues and organs.

Chapter 9

Ethics, Conservation, and Animal Welfare

Morals, protection, and creature government assistance are three interconnected mainstays of the advanced discussion encompassing mankind's relationship with the regular world. This intricate transaction frames the underpinning of our ethical obligations toward the climate and the animals that occupy it. In this 2000-word article, we will investigate the complex connection between morals, protection, and creature government assistance, digging into the moral rules that support our treatment of creatures and the job of preservation in safeguarding biodiversity.

1. **Morals and Creature Government assistance**

   Morals is the investigation of moral rules that oversee human way of behaving and the rightness or misleading quality of our activities. With regards to creature government assistance, moral contemplations assume a significant part in forming our mentalities and ways of behaving toward non-human creatures. Vital to this conversation is the subject of how we should treat creatures and whether they have inborn virtue.

   Anthropocentrism versus Non-Anthropocentrism

   The moral discussion about creature government assistance spins around two differentiating viewpoints: anthropocentrism and non-anthropocentrism. Anthropocentrism affirms that human interests ought to constantly overshadow the interests of creatures. This perspective has generally been predominant in Western way of thinking, yet it has confronted expanding analysis for its restricted thought of creatures' government assistance.

   Non-anthropocentrism, then again, contends that creatures have inborn worth and moral worth autonomously of their utility to people. This viewpoint envelops different moral structures, including basic entitlements, creature freedom, and ecological morals, that require a more comprehensive way to deal with thinking about the government assistance of every single conscious being.

Basic entitlements and Freedom

The idea of basic entitlements states that creatures, similar to people, have innate privileges that ought to be safeguarded, like the right to life, independence from anguish, and independence from double-dealing.

Unmistakable logician Peter Vocalist contends that species enrollment shouldn't decide a creature's ethical status, yet rather their ability to endure. Artist's utilitarian view stresses limiting anguish and expanding delight for every single aware being.

Additionally, the creature freedom development, as upheld by thinker Tom Regan, contends that creatures have inborn worth and privileges, not just instrumental incentive for people. They stress the guideline of "subject-of-a-day to day existence," which perceives that every individual creature has a remarkable point of view and interests that ought to be regarded and safeguarded.

Moral Contemplations in Creature Horticulture

Quite possibly of the most quarrelsome moral issue connected with creature government assistance is the treatment of creatures in horticulture. The cutting edge industrialized cultivating framework has raised critical worries with respect to the circumstances in which creatures are raised, their treatment, and the natural effect of huge scope creature farming.

In this unique situation, moral worries frequently rotate around processing plant cultivating, where creatures are exposed to confined and unfeeling circumstances, routine utilization of anti-microbials, and practices, for example, debeaking, tail docking, and the utilization of growth boxes for plants. Pundits contend that these practices compromise the government assistance and poise of creatures and bring up issues about the morals of delivering modest meat to the detriment of creature languishing.

2. **Preservation Morals**

Protection morals expands the moral thought from individual creatures to whole species, environments, and the safeguarding of biodiversity. It looks to address the ethical obligation people have in safeguarding the normal world and its occupants.

Biocentrism and Ecocentrism

Preservation morals can be extensively partitioned into two key points of view: biocentrism and ecocentrism. Biocentrism attests that all living creatures have characteristic worth and moral worth, not simply people. This point of view energizes the safeguarding of species and biological systems for the wellbeing of their own, perceiving the inborn worth of every species.

Ecocentrism takes a more extensive view, stressing the worth of whole biological systems and scenes, as well as the reliance of all living and non-living parts. This viewpoint perceives that biological systems have their own honesty and ought to be saved for the whole normal world.

Conservation versus Usage

Protection morals likewise wrestles with the pressure among conservation and use of regular assets. Preservationist morals contend for the assurance of wild regions, jeopardized species, and novel biological systems. This approach underlines the characteristic worth of nature and looks to limit human mediation in normal frameworks.

Conversely, utilitarian morals propose that people ought to use normal assets to address their issues, however do as such in a feasible and dependable way. This approach frequently includes offsetting monetary improvement with protection endeavors.

The Awfulness of the House

The awfulness of the house, an idea presented by Garrett Hardin, features the moral difficulties of asset the board in a common climate. In a situation where numerous people or gatherings approach a typical asset, they might exhaust it for their own potential benefit, at last prompting the asset's debasement or consumption.

Preservation morals resolves this issue by pushing for aggregate liability and feasible asset the board. It underlines the requirement for guidelines, collaboration, and dependable stewardship to forestall the awfulness of the house and safeguard regular assets for people in the future.

3. Exchange Between Morals, Protection, and Creature Government assistance

The exchange between morals, protection, and creature government assistance is apparent in various certifiable situations and difficulties. These three components cross and impact each other in different ways, prompting complex moral quandaries.

Imperiled Species Protection

The protection of imperiled species is a perfect representation of how these three standards unite. According to a moral point of view, the characteristic worth of individual creatures and the conservation of biodiversity drive endeavors to safeguard jeopardized species. The moral worry for creature government assistance underlines the need to guarantee that protection rehearses don't hurt or further jeopardize these species.

Preservation, thus, depends on the moral rule of protecting biodiversity, recognizing the characteristic worth of every species and their job inside biological systems. Adjusting the necessities of human networks with the government assistance and preservation of jeopardized species is a difficult moral problem that requires cautious thought.

Zoos and Hostage Rearing

The activity of zoos and hostage rearing projects fills in as another moral milestone where creature government assistance, protection, and morals converge. Zoos frequently house creatures for protection purposes, instructive open doors, and diversion. Pundits contend that imprisonment compromises the government assistance of creatures, particularly when their requirements are not sufficiently met.

Preservation morals guide these establishments to partake in species recuperation and rearing projects, fully intent on safeguarding jeopardized species and guaranteeing their endurance. Notwithstanding, moral worries emerge when creatures experience in bondage because of deficient space, ecological improvement, and social associations. Finding a harmony between protection endeavors and creature government assistance in these settings is a basic test.

Prize Hunting

Prize hunting presents a complex moral problem including creature government assistance, protection, and morals. Advocates contend that directed prize hunting can produce income for preservation endeavors and give impetuses to nearby networks to safeguard untamed life and their territories. Rivals, in any case, denounce prize hunting as uncaring and contend that it endangers the government assistance of individual creatures.

Moral points of view on prize hunting change, for certain people supporting the training for of preserving species and environments, while others censure it as ethically hostile. The exchange of preservation objectives, creature government assistance, and moral standards in this setting features the continuous discussion about whether prize hunting can be morally legitimate.

Intrusive Species The board

Overseeing intrusive species is another field where morals, protection, and creature government assistance meet. At the point when non-local species compromise native biological systems, preservation morals might uphold the evacuation of obtrusive species to safeguard neighborhood biodiversity. Be that as it may, moral worries emerge when these expulsion endeavors include hurting or killing individual creatures.

The moral issue in obtrusive species the board highlights the need to gauge the natural worth of individual creatures against the protection of environments. Preservation endeavors should adjust the government assistance of intrusive species with the assurance of local species and territories, featuring the intricate interchange between these standards.

9.1 Ethical Considerations in Animal Research

Creature research plays had an essential impact in progressing logical information, clinical medicines, and our comprehension of the regular world. In any case, the utilization of creatures in research has likewise been a wellspring of moral concern and discussion. This exposition investigates the moral contemplations encompassing creature research, including the rules that guide its utilization, the guidelines set up to safeguard creatures, and the continuous conversations about the harmony between logical advancement and creature government assistance.

1. **The Moral System**

The Utilitarian Viewpoint

Utilitarianism, a consequentialist moral system, assesses activities in light of their results and looks to boost in general prosperity. With regards to creature research, utilitarianism legitimizes the utilization of creatures when the likely advantages, like logical information or clinical progressions, offset the damages incurred for the creatures in question. Defenders contend that creature research prompts medicines and disclosures that benefit people, creatures, and the climate.

The Deontological Point of view

Deontological morals, then again, accentuate moral standards and obligations that ought to be observed no matter what the outcomes. In creature research, deontologists might contend that involving creatures for research objects is intrinsically off-base since it abuses the ethical obligation to approach all aware creatures with deference and try not to hurt. The Kantian rule of regarding people as closures in themselves as opposed to necessary evil lines up with this viewpoint.

The Goodness Morals Point of view

Goodness morals center around the personality of people and stress developing moral ideals. With regards to creature research, goodness morals would think about the ethics of sympathy, compassion, and obligation toward creatures. This point of view urges specialists to guarantee that creatures utilized in research are treated with graciousness and that their government assistance is a focal concern.

2. **Moral Standards in Creature Exploration**

The 3Rs: Substitution, Decrease, Refinement

The "3Rs" system is a core value in creature research morals. It represents Substitution, Decrease, and Refinement.

Substitution: The first "R" advocates for supplanting creature explores different avenues regarding non-creature choices whenever the situation allows. This guideline energizes the turn of events and utilization of strategies that can accomplish similar logical goals without utilizing creatures.

Decrease: The second "R" centers around limiting the quantity of creatures utilized. Specialists are urged to configuration tries that require less creatures while as yet accomplishing logical objectives.

Refinement: The third "R" underlines working on creature government assistance by refining trial methodology to limit agony and pain. This incorporates the utilization of sedation, help with discomfort, and better lodging conditions.

IACUCs and Moral Oversight

In numerous nations, Institutional Creature Care and Use Councils (IACUCs) are laid out to manage creature research. These boards of trustees are answerable for auditing research conventions, guaranteeing that analyses are directed as per moral and lawful norms, and making suggestions for refinement.

Informed Assent in Creature Exploration

In human examination, informed assent is a central moral necessity. In creature research, there is no immediate identical to informed assent, however the moral guideline of "informed hurt benefit examination" expects specialists to consider the likely damages to creatures against the possible advantages of the exploration cautiously. Straightforwardness and responsibility in this evaluation are fundamental.

3. **Moral Difficulties and Contentions**

Torment and Languishing

Quite possibly of the main moral worry in creature research is the expected aggravation and experiencing experienced by the creatures in question. The moral standard of limiting mischief highlights the significance of utilizing sedation, help with discomfort, and legitimate lodging to lessen creature languishing.

Speciesism

Speciesism is an idea that matches human separation in view of race, orientation, or different variables. With regards to creature research, it questions whether the interests and government assistance of creatures are given equivalent thought to those of people. Moral conversations frequently spin around whether the utilization of specific species is more adequate than others, possibly prompting the abuse of creatures considered less important or less like people.

The Issue of Assent

In human examination, informed assent is gotten from concentrate on members who can comprehend and consent to the exploration's terms. Creatures can't give assent, bringing up moral issues about their utilization in research. Moral contemplations are particularly mind boggling when the exploration includes profoundly conscious creatures like primates or dolphins.

The "Need" of Creature Exploration

A critical moral discussion encompasses the apparent need of creature research. Pundits contend that other options, for example, in vitro testing and PC demonstrating, are progressively reasonable and can diminish or supplant creature testing. That's what defenders battle, while these options are important, creature research stays fundamental for a few logical and clinical progressions.

4. **Moral Guidelines and Oversight**

The Three Rs in Regulation

Numerous nations have integrated the 3Rs standards into their regulation. Regulations and guidelines expect specialists to show how they have thought about the substitution, decrease, and refinement of creature use in their examinations.

Institutional Oversight

Institutional Creature Care and Use Panels (IACUCs) are answerable for auditing and supporting exploration conventions to guarantee they fulfill moral guidelines. Scientists should submit definite data about their proposed tests, including their defense and plans for limiting creature languishing.

Straightforwardness and Announcing

Straightforwardness is a significant part of moral oversight. Analysts are expected to give definite portrayals of their strategies, including the number and types of creatures utilized and the techniques in question. This data is ordinarily remembered for logical distributions and is fundamental for peer survey.

Moral Audit Sheets

Notwithstanding IACUCs, a few nations have laid out public or provincial moral survey sheets that assess and manage creature research. These sheets guarantee consistence with moral standards and applicable regulations.

5. **Options in contrast to Creature Exploration**

Endeavors are continuous to create and execute options in contrast to creature research, for example,

In Vitro Testing: Cell societies and tissue models can supplant a few creature tests, particularly in toxicology and medication improvement.

PC Displaying: Refined virtual experiences can supplant a few creature studies, especially in regions like pharmacokinetics and toxicology.

Organs-on-a-Chip: Microfluidic gadgets that impersonate the design and capability of human organs can supplant creature testing at times.

Human Workers: When achievable, human workers can partake in clinical preliminaries, diminishing the requirement for creature research.

Epidemiological Examinations: Breaking down information from human populaces can give important experiences into the impacts of specific elements without the requirement for creature studies.

9.2 The Legacy of Konrad Lorenz in Conservation

Konrad Lorenz, a spearheading Austrian ethologist and zoologist, left a significant heritage in the field of preservation that keeps on impacting how we comprehend and safeguard the normal world. His work on creature conduct, especially engraving and the investigation of ethology, gave bits of knowledge that aided shape present day protection endeavors. In this article, we will investigate the life and work of Konrad Lorenz, his commitments to the field of preservation, and what his thoughts keep on importance for the manner in which we approach natural life protection and ecological stewardship.

1. **The Life and Work of Konrad Lorenz**

Konrad Lorenz (1903-1989) was an unmistakable figure in the area of ethology, which is the logical investigation of creature conduct. Brought into the world in Austria, Lorenz at first concentrated on medication yet before long turned his concentration to science and zoology. He directed notable examination on the way of behaving of birds, especially geese and ducks, and is most popular for his work on engraving.

Engraving and Ethology

Lorenz's work on engraving altered how we might interpret how creatures learn and collaborate with their current circumstance. Engraving is an interaction by which youthful creatures structure solid, frequently irreversible, connections to the primary moving item they experience, ordinarily their folks. Lorenz's examinations on this peculiarity exhibited the meaning of early encounters in profoundly shaping a creature's way of behaving and social bonds.

Lorenz's Commitments to Preservation

Lorenz's commitments to the field of preservation were multi-layered. His bits of knowledge into creature conduct had critical ramifications for natural life the board and environment protection. A portion of the vital parts of his heritage in preservation include:

1. **Raising and Preservation**
   Lorenz's work on engraving worked on the progress of hostage rearing and renewed introduction programs for jeopardized species. By understanding how youthful creatures engrave on their guardians, progressives could bring creatures up in imprisonment while limiting human contact and engraving. This expanded the opportunities to effectively once again introduce hostage reared creatures into nature.

2. **Ethological Approach**
   Lorenz underlined the significance of concentrating on creatures in their common habitats to acquire a more profound comprehension of their way of behaving. This ethological approach affected moderates to consider the biological and social requirements of creatures while creating protection methodologies. His methodology underscored the meaning of saving flawless environments and tending to the conduct needs of creatures in nature.

3. **Moral Contemplations**

Lorenz was a vocal backer for the moral treatment of creatures, contending that people have an ethical obligation to secure and moderate species compromised by human exercises. His work on engraving and creature conduct helped feature the significance of limiting human impedance in the existences of wild creatures and regarding their natural worth.

II. Moral Ramifications of Lorenz's Work

Lorenz's work had significant moral ramifications for protection. His accentuation on getting it and regarding the normal way of behaving and social obligations of creatures tested conventional protection rehearses and supported a more caring methodology. A portion of the key moral contemplations enlivened by Lorenz's work include:

Empathetic Protection

Lorenz's exploration on engraving featured the profound and social necessities of creatures. This understanding urged moderates to take on a more humane methodology that thinks about the government assistance and mental prosperity of creatures in bondage and in nature.

Biological system Focused Protection

Lorenz's ethological approach underscored the significance of protecting environments in their normal state. This viewpoint perceived that preservation endeavors ought to stretch out past safeguarding individual species to shielding whole environments and their associated species.

Moral Treatment of Hostage Creatures

Lorenz's work affected the moral treatment of creatures in imprisonment, particularly in zoos and rearing projects. It prompted the advancement of further developed guidelines for lodging, care, and improvement to address the conduct and mental requirements of hostage creatures.

Ecological Morals

Lorenz's promotion for moral treatment of creatures stretched out to a more extensive thought of ecological morals. He contended for the moral obligation of people to safeguard the normal world and its occupants, stressing that the obliteration of biological systems and species is an ethical issue.

III. Lorenz's Effect on Current Protection

Konrad Lorenz's inheritance keeps on impacting present day preservation rehearses and the moral components of natural stewardship. His work has formed the accompanying key parts of contemporary preservation endeavors:

Ethology and Protection

The investigation of creature conduct stays a fundamental part of protection science. Ethologists attract upon Lorenz's experiences to comprehend how creatures associate with their surroundings, their social designs, and their conduct needs. This information illuminates protection methodologies, including living space safeguarding and the plan of safeguarded regions.

Hostage Rearing and Renewed introduction

Lorenz's work on engraving keeps on directing hostage rearing and renewed introduction programs. Traditionalists utilize his bits of knowledge to raise and plan creatures for discharge into the wild while limiting human obstruction and guaranteeing that the creatures can effectively adjust to their normal environment.

Empathetic Protection

The accentuation on empathetic protection, established in Lorenz's work, has built up forward movement in current preservation rehearses. It calls for moral contemplations that focus on the government assistance and pride of individual creatures, even with regards to more extensive species conservation.

Ecological Morals

Lorenz's promotion for ecological morals and the ethical obligation of people to safeguard the normal world has affected the more extensive protection development. This viewpoint has energized a more comprehensive way to deal with protection that tends to the interconnectedness of biological systems and perceives the inborn worth of every living being.

Training and Public Mindfulness

Lorenz's work plays likewise had an impact in raising public mindfulness about the moral components of protection. His works and talks promoted the possibility that protection isn't simply a logical undertaking however an ethical goal. This has added to the more extensive comprehension of the moral contemplations associated with natural life preservation.

IV. Difficulties and Reactions

While Lorenz's work fundamentally affects protection, it has not been without difficulties and reactions. A portion of the key worries include:

Humanoid attribution

Pundits have raised worries that Lorenz's work might prompt humanoid attribution, which includes ascribing human feelings and expectations to creatures. This can bring about false impressions of creature conduct and government assistance.

Misrepresentation

Lorenz's work, while pivotal, may distort the intricacy of creature conduct and social associations. Pundits contend that it is fundamental to consider the particular biological and developmental setting of every species while applying his bits of knowledge to preservation.

Restricted Application

Some have contended that Lorenz's work is generally appropriate to species with solid engraving conduct, like waterfowl, and may not be as straightforwardly applicable to other taxa. Moderates should consider the different exhibit of creature ways of behaving while creating procedures.

Moral Worries Before

Lorenz himself confronted analysis for his contribution with Nazi Germany during The Second Great War. He was an individual from the Nazi Party and the SA (Sturmabteilung), which prompted worries about his moral judgment and affiliations. This part of his past has brought up issues about the consistency of his moral positions, especially with regards to the treatment of people.

9.3 Promoting Animal Welfare Through Ethology

Ethology, the logical investigation of creature conduct, plays had a critical impact in advancing creature government assistance by giving significant bits of knowledge into the conduct, social, and mental requirements of creatures. Ethologists, through cautious perception and exploration, have added to how we might interpret how creatures experience and connect with their surroundings, which has expansive ramifications for working on their government assistance. In this paper, we will investigate the manners by which ethology adds to the advancement of creature government assistance, with an emphasis on key standards, the utilization of ethology in various settings, and the moral contemplations that emerge chasing better creature government assistance.

1. **Key Standards of Ethology in Advancing Creature Government assistance**
   Exact Perception

   Ethology depends on exact perception to grasp creature conduct. Analysts notice and record creatures in their common habitats or controlled settings to acquire bits of knowledge into their regular ways of behaving and social associations. This exact methodology permits researchers to foster a more significant comprehension of the necessities and inclinations of creatures.

   Near Examinations

   Relative examinations include looking at the way of behaving of various species, including people, to recognize shared characteristics and contrasts. By contrasting creature ways of behaving across species, ethologists can acquire a more extensive point of view on the development of conduct and the common requirements of creatures. This information can educate the advancement regarding government assistance measures for different species.

   Figuring out Creature Perception

   Ethologists examine the mental cycles of creatures to decide their ability for learning, critical thinking, and memory. This understanding is basic for planning proper advancement exercises in hostage conditions and working on the government assistance of creatures in both wild and homegrown settings.

   Ecological Advancement

   Ethological research has accentuated the significance of natural improvement in advancing creature government assistance. Enhancement includes giving creatures boosts and exercises that invigorate their regular ways of behaving and mental capacities. Ethologists help plan and execute advancement programs that upgrade the prosperity of creatures in imprisonment.

   Social Designs and Connections

   The investigation of creature social designs and connections is vital to ethology. Ethologists examine how creatures cooperate with each other, structure social securities, and impart. This information is fundamental for planning proper lodging and social conditions for creatures in imprisonment and overseeing untamed life populaces in their normal natural surroundings.

2. **Ethology in Various Settings**
   Zoos and Hostage Settings

Ethology has fundamentally affected how creatures are overseen in zoos, aquariums, and other hostage settings. By understanding the normal ways of behaving and social designs of creatures, ethologists assist with planning nooks that emulate the creatures' regular living spaces as intently as could really be expected. They additionally foster enhancement projects to keep creatures intellectually and truly locked in. The objective is to guarantee that creatures experience a great of life and that their regular ways of behaving are energized, decreasing the pressure of bondage.

Animal Cultivation and Cultivating

With regards to creature cultivation and horticulture, ethology assumes a urgent part in working on the government assistance of animals. Ethologists give bits of knowledge into the lodging conditions, social requirements, and conduct inclinations of creatures raised for food creation. This information advises the plan regarding more compassionate cultivating frameworks that focus on the government assistance of creatures and decrease pressure and languishing.

Untamed life Protection

Ethology is likewise applied to untamed life protection endeavors. Ethologists concentrate on the way of behaving and environment of imperiled species to foster techniques for their security and recuperation. This incorporates figuring out the living space prerequisites, taking care of ways of behaving, and social designs of untamed life populaces to guarantee that protection endeavors line up with the normal requirements of the species.

Friend Creature Government assistance

Ethology is fundamental in advancing the government assistance of friend creatures, like canines and felines. By concentrating on their way of behaving and discernment, ethologists assist with petting proprietors comprehend and meet the social and ecological necessities of their creatures. This prompts additional satisfying connections among people and their pets and upgrades the prosperity of buddy creatures.

3. **Moral Contemplations in Advancing Creature Government assistance through Ethology**

Regard for Regular Ways of behaving

One of the critical moral contemplations in ethology is the regard for a creature's normal ways of behaving and inclinations. Understanding and advancing these ways of behaving are fundamental for creature government assistance. This guideline directs the formation of conditions and the board rehearses that help regular ways of behaving, even in hostage settings.

Limiting Pressure and Languishing

Ethologists center around limiting pressure and experiencing in creatures. Seeing how animals respond to various circumstances and boosts empowers the advancement of measures to lessen wellsprings of stress, whether in imprisonment, on ranches, or in nature. This moral obligation to limiting enduring is essential to advancing creature government assistance.

Moral Utilization of Exploration Creatures

Ethologists directing examination on creatures should stick to moral principles. This incorporates getting important grants, limiting mischief to explore subjects, and guaranteeing that the exploration has a reasonable logical reason. The moral utilization of exploration creatures is basic to keeping up with the harmony between logical information and creature government assistance.

Moral Contemplations in Untamed life The board

With regards to natural life protection, ethologists face moral predicaments connected with mediations like movements, winnowing, or environment changes. Moral choices should be made by considering the prosperity of individual creatures, the preservation objectives, and the more extensive natural ramifications of moves initiated to safeguard an animal varieties or biological system.

Government funded Instruction and Mindfulness

Ethologists frequently take part in state funded training and mindfulness drives to advance moral contemplations in creature government assistance. By teaching the general population about the normal ways of behaving and needs of creatures, they engage people to settle on moral decisions with respect to creature government assistance, whether it includes pet possession, dietary decisions, or backing for preservation endeavors.

4. Ethology's Effect on Creature Government assistance

The effect of ethology on creature government assistance is apparent in different ways:

Further developed Lodging and Care

Ethological experiences have prompted huge upgrades in the lodging and care of animals in zoos, ranches, and research offices. By establishing conditions that help regular ways of behaving and giving improvement exercises, creatures experience less pressure and a better of life.

Upgraded Government assistance of Friend Creatures

Ethological research has worked on the government assistance of sidekick creatures. Understanding their conduct and mental requirements has prompted the advancement of preparing methods, socialization rehearses, and proper activity and improvement exercises that advantage pets and their proprietors.

Protection Achievement

Ethology has added to the outcome of preservation endeavors by assisting moderates with grasping the conduct prerequisites of jeopardized species. This information has educated the plan regarding safeguarded regions, hostage reproducing projects, and natural surroundings reclamation projects that better serve the necessities of the creatures in question.

Moral Customer Decisions

Public consciousness of ethological research has affected purchaser decisions connected with creature government assistance. Individuals are progressively looking for items that are obtained from frameworks that focus on the government assistance of creatures, like unfenced eggs or others consciously raised meat.

9.4 Balancing Science and Compassion

Adjusting science and sympathy is a significant and complex test that emerges across different spaces, from clinical exploration and natural life protection to horticulture and creature government assistance. The quest for logical information and the utilization of that information frequently include pursuing decisions that can affect the prosperity of people and environments. This exposition investigates the exchange among science and sympathy, looking at the moral, pragmatic, and philosophical contemplations that guide these choices and the manners by which society wrestles with the need to adjust the progression of information with moral and humane treatment.

1. **Science and Its Part in Propelling Information**
   The Logical Technique

   Science is an efficient course of request that looks to comprehend the normal world through perception, speculation testing, trial and error, and proof based ends. The logical strategy has been instrumental in propelling information and tending to a large number of inquiries and difficulties. It has prompted astounding revelations in fields like medication, innovation, and natural science.

   Moral Contemplations in Exploration

   While the logical technique is priceless in propelling information, moral contemplations are fundamental to logical examination. Moral rules and guidelines are set up to guarantee that examination is led in a way that regards the privileges and government assistance of people, creatures, and environments. These moral contemplations are grounded in standards of regard, usefulness, and equity.

2. **Sympathy and Its Part in Moral Navigation**
   Sympathy Characterized

   Sympathy is the compassionate worry for the torment or prosperity of others, be they people, creatures, or the climate. It is established in the comprehension that all conscious creatures have interests, wants, and an ability to endure. Empathy drives people and social orders to act in manners that ease enduring and advance prosperity.

   Moral Systems

   Empathy is a central guideline in different moral structures, including utilitarianism, deontology, and temperance morals. Utilitarianism accentuates expanding generally speaking prosperity and diminishing affliction. Deontological morals, like Kantian standards, accentuate the ethical obligation to approach all people with deference and graciousness. Excellence morals supports the development of moral ideals, including empathy, for the purpose of directing moral navigation.

3. **Adjusting Science and Sympathy in Clinical Exploration**
Creature Testing

Clinical exploration frequently includes the utilization of creatures for tests, for example, drug testing and the investigation of illnesses. This training is morally perplexing, as it adjusts the headway of logical information with empathy for the government assistance of creatures. Moral rules in creature research expect specialists to limit hurt, use choices whenever the situation allows, and guarantee that examination has a reasonable logical and clinical reason.

Moral Contemplations in Clinical Preliminaries

In clinical exploration including people, clinical preliminaries bring up moral issues about the harmony between logical progression and sympathy for preliminary members. Moral contemplations incorporate informed assent, risk-benefit appraisals, and the prosperity of members. Finding some kind of harmony is fundamental to guarantee that the advantages of logical exploration offset the expected damages.

4. **Adjusting Science and Empathy in Untamed life Preservation**
Preservation Problems

Natural life preservation frequently includes tough decisions, for example, populace control, living space the board, and the administration of obtrusive species. Adjusting the interests of natural life populaces and environments with moral contemplations requires cautious navigation. Moral systems, as natural morals, require an all encompassing methodology that regards the inborn worth of environments and considers the prosperity of individual creatures.

Jeopardized Species The board

Jeopardized species the board embodies the strain among science and empathy. Choices with respect to the movement, separating, or environment alterations fundamental for species recuperation can morally challenge. Traditionalists should gauge the prosperity of individual creatures against the protection objectives and biological outcomes of their activities.

5. **Adjusting Science and Empathy in Farming**
Animal Government assistance in Cultivating

Farming countenances the moral test of adjusting the need to create nourishment for a developing populace with worries for animal government assistance. Escalated cultivating rehearses have raised worries about the treatment of animals creatures. Moral contemplations request that creatures be brought up in conditions that limit enduring and advance prosperity.

This has prompted developments upholding for empathetic cultivating rehearses and an emphasis on sympathy for creatures in farming.

Feasible Agribusiness

Adjusting science and empathy in agribusiness stretches out to the natural effect of cultivating rehearses. Feasible agribusiness looks to adjust the logical comprehension of harvest yields and effective creation with empathy for the climate. This incorporates lessening the utilization of hurtful synthetic substances, rationing assets, and alleviating the environmental outcomes of agribusiness.

6. **Adjusting Science and Empathy in Natural Stewardship**
Biodiversity Protection

Biodiversity protection frequently includes hard choices, for example, overseeing environments, controlling obtrusive species, or directing untamed life populace control. Adjusting logical information about biological systems with sympathy for individual creatures and environments is a fragile errand. Moral standards require the conservation of biodiversity while regarding the prosperity of individual life forms.

Natural surroundings Safeguarding

Adjusting science and empathy in natural stewardship stretches out to environment protection. Preservation endeavors expect to safeguard regular living spaces while limiting damage to biological systems and the species inside them. Moral contemplations highlight the significance of considering the natural necessities of territories and the prosperity of all living beings in the environment.

7. **Public Mindfulness and Training**

Public mindfulness and schooling assume an essential part in finding some kind of harmony among science and empathy. By illuminating people in general about the moral contemplations in different spaces, including clinical examination, natural life preservation, agribusiness, and ecological stewardship, society can go with additional educated decisions. Public strain can likewise impact the advancement of additional merciful approaches and practices in these fields.

8. **Moral Administration and Navigation**

Moral administration and direction are significant in adjusting science and empathy. Pioneers in science, industry, and government should consider the moral ramifications of their choices. This requires considering the prosperity of people and biological systems while progressing logical information and tending to commonsense difficulties.

Chapter 10

Beyond Lorenz: Contemporary Ethology

Ethology, the logical investigation of creature conduct, has a rich history and a brilliant future. While Konrad Lorenz, Nikolaas Tinbergen, and Karl von Frisch established the groundwork for ethology during the twentieth 100 years, the field has advanced altogether from that point forward. Contemporary ethology envelops a great many methodologies, philosophies, and exploration points, mirroring the interdisciplinary idea of this part of science. In this paper, we will investigate the improvements in contemporary ethology, including the development of exploration spaces, new systems, and the combination of present day advancements. We will likewise analyze the more extensive ramifications of contemporary ethological research for how we might interpret the regular world and our own species.

Extending Exploration Areas

Contemporary ethology has widened its examination spaces, moving past the conventional spotlight on creature conduct to envelop different subjects and species. This development mirrors the field's acknowledgment of the interconnectedness of every living life form and the significance of concentrating on many ways of behaving and their natural settings. A portion of the critical areas of exploration in contemporary ethology include:

Creature Correspondence: The investigation of creature correspondence has seen huge progressions, with specialists examining vocalizations and visual signs as well as synthetic, electrical, and material types of correspondence. Research has stretched out to species-explicit dialects and the advancement of correspondence frameworks.

Social Way of behaving: Ethologists inspect different parts of social way of behaving, including participation, animosity, and the arrangement of social pecking orders. Research has uncovered the perplexing elements of creature social orders and their versatile importance.

Mental Ethology: The investigation of creature comprehension has acquired noticeable quality, zeroing in on creatures' psychological cycles, critical abilities to think, memory, and learning. Specialists investigate the mental limits of a large number of animal categories, from primates and cetaceans to birds and even bugs.

Conduct Nature: Contemporary ethology puts areas of strength for an on the environmental setting of conduct. Specialists explore how natural variables, including predation, asset accessibility, and environmental change, impact creature conduct and methods for surviving.

Human Ethology: Ethological standards have additionally been applied to the investigation of human way of behaving. Human ethology looks at our transformative history, social collaborations, and versatile ways of behaving with regards to current cultures.

Systemic Headways

Progressions in research philosophies play had a critical impact in molding contemporary ethology. These improvements have empowered analysts to acquire further bits of knowledge into creature conduct and to investigate new roads of study. A portion of the critical strategic progressions in contemporary ethology include:

Field Studies: Ethologists progressively lead field concentrates on in common habitats, permitting them to notice creatures in their normal territories. This approach gives significant experiences into the environmental setting of conduct and limits the likely impact of bondage.

Innovation Mix: Present day innovation, including GPS following, remote detecting, and camera traps, has changed information assortment in ethology. Analysts can accumulate information all the more productively and unpretentiously, even in remote or testing conditions.

Sub-atomic Strategies: Hereditary and sub-atomic apparatuses have been integrated into ethological research. DNA investigation can assist analysts with distinguishing people, concentrate on relatedness, and follow the hereditary premise of conduct.

Neuroethology: The area of neuroethology looks at the brain components basic creature conduct. Scientists use methods, for example, neuroimaging and electrophysiology to explore the brain circuits and mind locales liable for explicit ways of behaving.

Exploratory Controls: Ethologists utilize controlled trials to control explicit factors and test theories about conduct. These tests permit scientists to lay out causal connections and gain a more profound comprehension of social instruments.

Resident Science: Resident science projects including volunteers and local area support have become more common. These drives empower the assortment of enormous datasets and add to how we might interpret creature conduct and dispersion.

Combination of Current Advances

Contemporary ethology use current innovations to propel how we might interpret creature conduct. A few mechanical developments fundamentally affect the field:

GPS Following and Telemetry: The utilization of GPS gadgets and telemetry frameworks permits scientists to follow the development and conduct of creatures in nature. This innovation has revealed insight into relocation designs, scrounging techniques, and environment use.

Remote Detecting: Satellite symbolism, remote detecting innovation, and robots give significant information to concentrating on creatures in their regular habitats. These devices are especially valuable for observing natural life populaces and environments.

Camera Traps: Camera traps have changed the investigation of slippery and night-time creatures. These movement enacted cameras catch pictures and recordings of natural life without direct human perception, giving experiences into conduct and dispersion.

Bioacoustics: Advances in bioacoustics innovation have extended how we might interpret creature correspondence. Scientists utilize specific amplifiers and sound examination programming to record and investigate creature vocalizations.

Hereditary Investigation: DNA examination procedures have become fundamental for ethologists concentrating on relatedness, populace hereditary qualities, and the hereditary premise of conduct. DNA fingerprinting and sequencing strategies assist with distinguishing people and their family connections.

Wearable Innovation: Scaled down sensors and trackers can be appended to creatures, permitting analysts to screen their physiology, conduct, and associations. This innovation gives nitty gritty bits of knowledge into the regular routines of creatures.

Transdisciplinary Approaches

Contemporary ethology progressively embraces transdisciplinary approaches, overcoming any barrier between various logical disciplines. Coordinated efforts between ethologists, biologists, neuroscientists, geneticists, and different specialists have enhanced how we might interpret creature conduct by thinking about a great many elements. These interdisciplinary methodologies include:

Ethoecology: Ethoecology centers around the connection between creature conduct and the climate. By incorporating biological and ethological research, researchers can more readily comprehend how conduct is molded by natural settings.

Neuroethology: This field investigates the brain premise of creature conduct, underscoring the connection between the cerebrum and conduct. It joins the procedures of neuroscience and ethology to explore the brain instruments answerable for explicit ways of behaving.

Transformative Ethology: Developmental ethologists concentrate on the advancement of conduct and what it is meant for by regular determination. This transdisciplinary approach consolidates standards from ethology, transformative science, and hereditary qualities to make sense of the versatile meaning of ways of behaving.

Social Ethology: Social ethology analyzes the social variety in creature conduct inside and between populaces. This approach thinks about how learned ways of behaving, customs, and social practices can impact the development of conduct.

Suggestions for Preservation

Contemporary ethology significantly affects natural life protection and the safeguarding of biodiversity:

Living space The board: Understanding the way of behaving of compromised or jeopardized species illuminates natural surroundings the executives and preservation endeavors. Information on rummaging propensities, movement courses, and reproducing ways of behaving helps plan powerful protection plans.

Populace Checking: Conduct information gathered through present day advances and field perceptions empower the observing of natural life populaces. Preservationists can follow populace size, regenerative achievement, and the effect of ecological changes on conduct.

Preservation Brain research: Incorporating mental standards with ethology, protection brain science investigates human-creature communications, perspectives, and inspirations. This information can impact public help for preservation drives and advance mindful way of behaving toward natural life.

Human-Untamed life Struggle Moderation: Ethological bits of knowledge into creature conduct can illuminate techniques for alleviating clashes among people and natural life. Understanding the way of behaving of species that come into contact with human settlements is urgent for limiting negative communications.

Suggestions for Grasping Human Way of behaving

Contemporary ethology additionally has suggestions for how we might interpret human way of behaving:

Developmental Brain research: By concentrating on the way of behaving of different creatures and taking into account our common transformative history, contemporary ethology adds to the field of transformative brain research. This approach investigates what genealogical ways of behaving and transformations have meant for human brain science and social elements.

Social Advancement: Experiences from social ethology and the investigation of creature customs have impacted the field of social development in people. Scientists analyze the transmission of ways of behaving, customs, and social practices among human populaces.

Preservation of Human Way of behaving: The investigation of creature conduct can move rehearses that advance economical and dependable human way of behaving, especially with regards to asset use, collaboration, and social association.

10.1 Modern Advances in the Study of Animal Behavior

The investigation of creature conduct, known as ethology, has seen critical advances in late many years, powered by developing examination strategies, interdisciplinary cooperation, and mechanical developments. Ethologists look to figure out the complicated cooperations, variations, and mental cycles that administer how creatures explore their surroundings, convey, replicate, and get by. In this paper, we will investigate the cutting edge progresses in the investigation of creature conduct, going from the combination of genomics and neurobiology to the utilization of state of the art innovation and the bits of knowledge acquired from interdisciplinary cooperation.

These improvements have extended how we might interpret creature conduct as well as given significant applications in regions like protection, human brain research, and the headway of computerized reasoning.

Genomics and Conduct Hereditary qualities

The joining of genomics and conduct hereditary qualities has changed how we might interpret the hereditary underpinnings of creature conduct. Analysts can now investigate the hereditary premise of conduct by looking at the qualities and subatomic pathways that impact explicit characteristics and propensities.

1. **Competitor Quality Methodologies:** Studies have recognized applicant qualities related with different ways of behaving, like searching, mating inclinations, and hostility. For instance, the "rummaging quality" in bumble bees impacts their searching way of behaving and task specialization inside the hive.
2. **Quantitative Hereditary qualities:** Quantitative hereditary qualities empowers analysts to assess the heritability of explicit ways of behaving inside populaces. This approach unwinds the hereditary commitments to complex qualities and their advancement.
3. **Social Epigenetics:** Epigenetic alterations, like DNA methylation, have been connected to the guideline of conduct. Understanding how epigenetics impacts conduct is a promising road in current ethology.

Neurobiology and Conduct

Headways in neurobiology have extended how we might interpret the brain systems that underlie creature conduct. Specialists can explore mind structures, brain circuits, and synapse frameworks to reveal the connections between the cerebrum and conduct.

1. **Neuroethology:** The area of neuroethology investigates the brain premise of conduct. Analysts use procedures like neuroimaging and electrophysiology to distinguish the brain processes and designs answerable for explicit ways of behaving.
2. **Neurogenomics:** Advances in genomics have empowered scientists to concentrate on the hereditary premise of brain improvement and capability, revealing insight into the connection among qualities and conduct.

3. **Neurochemical Flagging:** Ethologists explore the job of synapses, neuropeptides, and chemicals in conduct. For instance, the investigation of oxytocin and vasopressin has given experiences into social holding in creatures.

Conduct Biology

Present day ethology has areas of strength for an on social environment, stressing the biological setting wherein creature conduct happens. Scientists investigate how ecological elements, asset accessibility, predation hazard, and environmental change impact creature conduct and methods for surviving.

1. **Ideal Rummaging Hypothesis:** Ideal searching hypothesis tries to comprehend how creatures boost their energy gain while limiting expenses. This hypothesis has been applied to different parts of conduct, including prey choice, food reserving, and relocation.
2. **Parental Speculation Hypothesis:** Parental venture hypothesis investigates the compromises between the assets dispensed to propagation, care of posterity, and self-upkeep. It has suggestions for grasping mating methodologies, mate choice, and regenerative way of behaving.
3. **Game Hypothesis:** Game hypothesis is utilized to display social associations and clashes between creatures. Analysts apply this way to deal with concentrate on participation, animosity, and the development of social way of behaving.

Mental Ethology

The investigation of creature cognizance, known as mental ethology, has acquired conspicuousness in current ethology. Analysts examine creatures' psychological cycles, critical thinking skills, memory, and learning. The experiences acquired from mental ethology challenge conventional perspectives on creature knowledge.

1. **Instrument Use and Critical thinking:** The investigation of hardware use and critical thinking has uncovered the mental complexity of creatures like chimpanzees, dolphins, and birds. Specialists use puzzles and exploratory arrangements to survey creatures' capacities to adjust and advance.
2. **Memory and Learning:** Ethologists look at the job of memory and learning in creature conduct. Traditional and operant molding tests give significant data about the capacity of creatures to relate improvements and adjust their way of behaving appropriately.
3. **Mathematical Insight:** Ongoing exploration investigates creatures' mathematical cognizance, including their capacity to figure out amount and perform fundamental number-crunching assignments. This field offers bits of knowledge into the mental limits of different species.

Interdisciplinary Cooperation

Contemporary ethology advances interdisciplinary cooperation, empowering scientists from different fields to cooperate and share bits of knowledge into creature conduct. This approach has enhanced the investigation of conduct by incorporating various viewpoints and philosophies.

1. **Ethoecology:** Ethoecology analyzes the collaboration between creature conduct and the climate. Specialists incorporate biological and ethological examination to comprehend how conduct is molded by natural settings.
2. **Neuroethology:** The area of neuroethology joins standards from neuroscience and ethology to investigate the brain systems hidden creature conduct. This interdisciplinary methodology uncovers the brain circuits and cerebrum areas liable for explicit ways of behaving.
3. **Social Ethology:** Social ethology examines the social variety in creature conduct inside and between populaces. This approach thinks about how learned ways of behaving, customs, and social practices can impact the advancement of conduct.

Current Innovation

Current innovation has upset the investigation of creature conduct, furnishing scientists with amazing assets for information assortment, examination, and perception.

1. **GPS Following and Telemetry:** GPS gadgets and telemetry frameworks empower analysts to follow the development and conduct of creatures in nature. This innovation has uncovered movement designs, searching procedures, and natural surroundings use.
2. **Remote Detecting:** Satellite symbolism, remote detecting innovation, and robots give important information to concentrating on creatures in their common habitats. These apparatuses are especially helpful for checking untamed life populaces and territories.
3. **Camera Traps:** Camera traps have changed the investigation of slippery and nighttime creatures. These movement enacted cameras catch pictures and recordings of natural life without direct human perception, giving bits of knowledge into conduct and dissemination.
4. **Hereditary Examination:** DNA investigation methods have become fundamental for ethologists concentrating on relatedness, populace hereditary qualities, and the hereditary premise of conduct. DNA fingerprinting and sequencing techniques assist with distinguishing people and their family connections.
5. **Wearable Innovation:** Scaled down sensors and trackers can be appended to creatures, permitting specialists to screen their physiology, conduct, and collaborations. This innovation gives nitty gritty bits of knowledge into the regular routines of creatures.

Suggestions for Protection

The advances in the investigation of creature conduct have significant ramifications for untamed life protection and the safeguarding of biodiversity:

1. **Natural surroundings The board:** Understanding the way of behaving of undermined or jeopardized species illuminates living space the executives and preservation endeavors. Information on scrounging propensities, relocation courses, and reproducing ways of behaving helps plan successful protection plans.
2. **Populace Checking:** Social information gathered through current advancements and field perceptions empower the observing of natural life populaces. Protectionists can follow populace size, conceptive achievement, and the effect of natural changes on conduct.
3. **Preservation Brain research:** Coordinating mental standards with ethology, protection brain science investigates human-creature associations, perspectives, and inspirations. This information can impact public help for preservation drives and advance mindful way of behaving toward untamed life.
4. **Human-Untamed life Struggle Moderation:** Ethological experiences into creature conduct can illuminate techniques for alleviating clashes among people and natural life. Understanding the way of behaving of species that come into contact with human settlements is essential for limiting negative collaborations.

Suggestions for Grasping Human Way of behaving

Contemporary ethology likewise has suggestions for how we might interpret human way of behaving:

1. **Transformative Brain science:** By concentrating on the way of behaving of different creatures and taking into account our common developmental history, contemporary ethology adds to the field of transformative brain science.
   This approach investigates what hereditary ways of behaving and transformations have meant for human brain research and social elements.
2. **Social Development:** Experiences from social ethology and the investigation of creature customs have affected the field of social advancement in people. Scientists inspect the transmission of ways of behaving, customs, and social practices among human populaces.
3. **Protection of Human Way of behaving:** The investigation of creature conduct can rouse rehearses that advance maintainable and mindful human way of behaving, especially with regards to asset use, participation, and social association.

10.2 The Integration of Ethology with Other Disciplines

Ethology, the logical investigation of creature conduct, has a rich history and a solid practice of interdisciplinary cooperation. Throughout the long term, ethology has extended its viewpoints by coordinating bits of knowledge and procedures from different disciplines. This interdisciplinary methodology has improved how we might interpret creature conduct, prompting leap forwards in regions like neurobiology, environment, hereditary qualities, and brain research. In this article, we will investigate the coordination of ethology with different disciplines, featuring the manners by which this joint effort has widened the field, extended our insight into creature conduct, and yielded important applications in assorted settings.

Ethoecology: The Interchange of Ethology and Biology

One of the most critical and persevering through interdisciplinary joint efforts inside ethology is the mix with nature, coming about in a subfield known as ethoecology. Ethoecology investigates the perplexing exchange between creature conduct and the climate, stressing the environmental setting where ways of behaving happen. This approach perceives that the way of behaving of creatures is unpredictably connected to the natural surroundings they occupy, the assets accessible to them, and the cooperations with different species.

1. **Living space Determination:** Ethoecologists examine how creatures pick their territories, investigating the elements that impact their choice, like food accessibility, haven, and hunter evasion. Understanding these choices is fundamental for untamed life preservation and biological system the executives.

2. **Rummaging Conduct:** The investigation of creature scavenging conduct inside the setting of ethoecology looks at how creatures find, catch, and interaction food assets. This examination reveals insight into energy spending plans, taking care of procedures, and the effect of scrounging conduct on environments.

3. **Relocation Examples:** Ethoecologists concentrate on the movement examples of creatures, like birds, vertebrates, and marine species, with an emphasis on the environmental drivers and outcomes of these developments. This exploration illuminates protection endeavors and features the significance of living space conservation along relocation courses.

4. **Predation and Against Hunter Methodologies:** The hunter prey collaborations and hostile to hunter systems of creatures are key in ethoecology. Specialists explore the ways of behaving and variations that creatures utilize to avoid predation and how these procedures shift in various environmental settings.

The mix of ethology with biology has yielded important experiences into the complicated elements of biological systems and how creature conduct adds to environmental steadiness. This cooperation is fundamental for tending to ecological difficulties, monitoring biodiversity, and overseeing normal assets.

Neuroethology: Crossing over Conduct and Neuroscience

Neuroethology is a subfield of ethology that spotlights on the brain premise of creature conduct. It overcomes any barrier among conduct and neuroscience, investigating the brain circuits, designs, and cycles that underlie explicit ways of behaving. By incorporating standards from the two fields, neuroethologists try to uncover the systems that drive conduct.

1. **Brain Circuits:** Neuroethologists examine the brain circuits answerable for ways of behaving like romance, route, mating, and correspondence. This exploration gives a more profound comprehension of the particular pathways in the cerebrum that control these ways of behaving.
2. **Synapse Frameworks:** The job of synapses in creature conduct is a noticeable subject in neuroethology. Analysts inspect how substances like dopamine, serotonin, and acetylcholine impact conduct and adjust brain movement.
3. **Tangible Discernment:** Neuroethology investigates how creatures see and interaction tactile data. This examination explains how creatures identify boosts, from sound and light to synthetics and vibrations, and how these insights drive conduct.
4. **Development of Brain Components:** Near examinations inside neuroethology explore how brain systems have advanced across various species. This approach gives experiences into the versatile meaning of explicit ways of behaving and the hereditary premise of brain qualities.

The mix of ethology with neuroscience has significant ramifications for figuring out the connections among mind and conduct. This joint effort upgrades our insight into the brain underpinnings of creature activities, from complex mating customs to perplexing route and correspondence.

Social Hereditary qualities: Disentangling the Hereditary Premise of Conduct

The reconciliation of social hereditary qualities with ethology has reformed how we might interpret the hereditary premise of creature conduct. Specialists currently investigate the qualities, sub-atomic pathways, and epigenetic systems that impact explicit ways of behaving.

1. **Applicant Quality Methodologies:** Ethologists team up with geneticists to recognize competitor qualities related with ways of behaving like mate decision, searching, and animosity. For instance, the "rummaging quality" in bumble bees impacts their scavenging conduct and assignment specialization.
2. **Quantitative Hereditary qualities:** The investigation of quantitative hereditary qualities permits specialists to appraise the heritability of explicit ways of behaving inside populaces. This approach unwinds the hereditary commitments to complex qualities and their advancement.
3. **Social Epigenetics:** Conduct epigenetics researches how epigenetic adjustments, like DNA methylation, control conduct. This exploration features the powerful interchange among hereditary qualities and natural effects on conduct.

The coordination of social hereditary qualities with ethology broadens how we might interpret the hereditary determinants of conduct and the heritability of explicit attributes. It gives experiences into the hereditary variety inside populaces and the transformative elements of conduct.

Human Ethology: Overcoming any barrier Among Human and Creature Conduct

Human ethology investigates the way of behaving of people with regards to transformative standards and relative examinations. This interdisciplinary methodology applies ethological ideas and techniques to the investigation of human way of behaving, revealing insight into our transformative legacy and social connections.

1. **Developmental Brain research:** Human ethology adds to the field of transformative brain research, which looks at human conduct with regards to our transformative history. This approach investigates what genealogical ways of behaving and variations have meant for human brain science, discernment, and social elements.

2. **Social Development:** Bits of knowledge from human ethology illuminate the review regarding social advancement in people. Analysts research the transmission of ways of behaving, customs, and social practices inside and between human populaces, taking into account the job of learned ways of behaving in social change.

3. **Protection of Human Way of behaving:** Human ethology can move rehearses that advance feasible and capable human way of behaving, especially with regards to asset use, collaboration, and social association. This approach stresses the significance of grasping human ways of behaving that influence the climate.

The joining of human ethology with the investigation of creature conduct highlights the common transformative rules that oversee conduct across species. This joint effort upgrades how we might interpret human conduct with regards to our organic and social legacy.

Innovation Coordination: Altering Information Assortment

The coordination of cutting edge innovation with ethology has altered information assortment and examination, empowering scientists to notice and screen creature conduct all the more proficiently and unpretentiously.

1. **GPS Following and Telemetry:** The utilization of GPS gadgets and telemetry frameworks permits analysts to follow the development and conduct of creatures in nature. This innovation has revealed insight into relocation designs, searching systems, and environment use.

2. **Remote Detecting:** Satellite symbolism, remote detecting innovation, and robots give important information to concentrating on creatures in their

common habitats. These devices are especially valuable for checking untamed life populaces and natural surroundings.

3. **Camera Traps:** Camera traps have changed the investigation of subtle and night-time creatures. These movement actuated cameras catch pictures and recordings of untamed life without direct human perception, giving bits of knowledge into conduct and dispersion.

4. **Hereditary Investigation:** DNA examination procedures have become funda-mental for ethologists concentrating on relatedness, populace hereditary quali-ties, and the hereditary premise of conduct. DNA fingerprinting and sequencing techniques assist with recognizing people and their family connections.

5. **Wearable Innovation:** Scaled down sensors and trackers can be connected to creatures, permitting specialists to screen their physiology, conduct, and col-laborations. This innovation gives itemized bits of knowledge into the regular routines of creatures.

The mix of innovation with ethology has extended the extent of examination, empowering scientists to gather enormous datasets, lead long haul perceptions, and investigate creature conduct in remote or testing conditions.

10.3 The Ongoing Quest for Understanding Animal Ways

The investigation of creature conduct, or ethology, has been a continuous mission for understanding the manners by which creatures explore their surroundings, impart, imitate, and get by. From the early work of trailblazers like Konrad Lorenz, Nikolaas Tinbergen, and Karl von Frisch to the contemporary headways in ethology, specialists have gained exceptional headway in unwinding the intricacies of creature conduct. This continuous mission for understanding creature ways includes a multidisciplinary approach that coordinates bits of knowledge from fields like biology, neurobiology, hereditary qualities, and brain research. In this article, we will investigate the advance-ment of ethology, contemporary examination in the field, and the ramifications of our continuous journey for figuring out the way of behaving of creatures.

1. **The Development of Ethology**

1. **Essential Work of Early Ethologists**

   The foundations of ethology can be followed back to the mid twentieth century when specialists like Konrad Lorenz, Nikolaas Tinbergen, and Karl von Frisch made weighty commitments to the field. Their work established the ground-work for the investigation of creature conduct.

   Konrad Lorenz: Lorenz's spearheading research centered around the engraving conduct in birds. He found that specific creatures, similar to goslings, have a basic period during which they structure solid connections to the primary moving item they see, ordinarily their mom. This revelation changed how we might interpret early learning and social connection in creatures.

Nikolaas Tinbergen: Tinbergen's exploration incorporated many points, from the romance ways of behaving of stickleback fish to the settling conduct of digger wasps. He presented the idea of the "Four Whys" to grasp conduct, accentuating the significance of researching the capability, causation, advancement, and development of ways of behaving.

Karl von Frisch: Von Frisch's spearheading work included the investigation of honey bee correspondence and route. He interpreted the dance language of honey bees, uncovering how they impart the area of food sources to their hive mates through perplexing moves. Von Frisch's exploration procured him a Nobel Prize.

2. **The Rise of Contemporary Ethology**

The mid-twentieth century saw the rise of contemporary ethology, set apart by an extended spotlight on creature conduct in normal settings and a combination of different logical disciplines.

Conduct Nature: Ethologists started to investigate the biological setting of creature conduct, taking into account how ecological elements, asset accessibility, predation hazard, and environment impact conduct. Conduct biology accentuated the versatile meaning of ways of behaving inside their natural specialties.

Mental Ethology: The investigation of creature insight acquired unmistakable quality, zeroing in on creatures' psychological cycles, critical abilities to think, memory, and learning. Analysts perceived that creatures have complex mental capacities and adjust their conduct in light of their current circumstance.

Neuroethology: Ethologists overcame any barrier among conduct and neuroscience, investigating the brain systems that underlie explicit ways of behaving. Neuroethology researches the brain circuits, cerebrum designs, and synapse frameworks that oversee creature conduct.

Human Ethology: Ethologists applied the standards of ethology to the investigation of human way of behaving, looking at our transformative history, social associations, and versatile ways of behaving with regards to current cultures. Human ethology added to fields like developmental brain science and social advancement.

II. **Contemporary Exploration in Ethology**

1. **Social Nature**

Contemporary ethologists keep on investigating the many-sided connections among creatures and their surroundings, revealing insight into how ways of behaving have developed to upgrade endurance and proliferation.

Ideal Rummaging Hypothesis: Ethologists apply ideal scrounging hypothesis to comprehend how creatures expand their energy gain while limiting costs in the quest for food. This hypothesis has been instrumental in making sense of prey determination, scavenging methodologies, and food storing.

Parental Speculation Hypothesis: The investigation of parental venture investigates the compromises between assets dispensed to proliferation, care of posterity, and self-support. This hypothesis enlightens the development of mating methodologies, mate determination, and conceptive way of behaving.

Game Hypothesis: Ethologists utilize game hypothesis to display social associations and clashes between creatures. This approach makes sense of the advancement of agreeable ways of behaving, hostility, and social designs.

2. **Mental Ethology**

Research in mental ethology keeps on uncovering the mental capacities of creatures and their ability to adjust and advance.

Apparatus Use and Critical thinking: Ethologists concentrate on device use and critical thinking in different species, revealing the mental complexity of creatures like chimpanzees, dolphins, and birds. Analysts use puzzles and trial arrangements to survey creatures' capacities to adjust and advance.

Memory and Learning: The job of memory and learning in creature conduct is an unmistakable focal point of mental ethology. Scientists research the capacity of creatures to relate improvements, gain from encounters, and adjust their conduct in light of previous occasions.

Mathematical Discernment: Late examination investigates creatures' mathematical perception, including their capacity to grasp amount and perform essential number-crunching undertakings. This field offers experiences into the mental limits of different species.

3. **Neuroethology**

The area of neuroethology keeps on unwinding the brain premise of creature conduct, uncovering the complexities of brain circuits and components that underlie explicit ways of behaving.

Brain Circuits: Analysts examine the brain circuits answerable for ways of behaving like romance, route, mating, and correspondence. This examination gives a more profound comprehension of the particular pathways in the mind that control these ways of behaving.

Synapse Frameworks: The job of synapses in creature conduct is an unmistakable point in neuroethology. Specialists analyze how substances like dopamine, serotonin, and acetylcholine impact conduct and tweak brain movement.

Tangible Discernment: Neuroethology investigates how creatures see and cycle tactile data. This examination explains how creatures identify improvements, from sound and light to synthetic substances and vibrations, and how these discernments drive conduct.

4. **Human Ethology**

The utilization of ethological standards to the investigation of human conduct keeps on giving experiences into the transformative legacy and social cooperations of people.

Developmental Brain science: By concentrating on the way of behaving of different creatures and taking into account our common transformative history, human ethology adds to the field of developmental brain research. This approach investigates what genealogical ways of behaving and variations have meant for human brain science and social elements.

Social Development: Bits of knowledge from social ethology and the investigation of creature customs have affected the field of social advancement in people. Specialists inspect the transmission of ways of behaving, customs, and social practices among human populaces.

Protection of Human Way of behaving: Human ethology can rouse rehearses that advance practical and capable human way of behaving, especially with regards to asset use, collaboration, and social association. This approach underlines the significance of figuring out human ways of behaving that influence the climate.

III. Ramifications of the Continuous Mission for Figuring out Creature Ways

1. **Protection**

   The continuous mission for understanding creature conduct has huge ramifications for untamed life protection and the safeguarding of biodiversity.

   Environment The board: Ethological experiences into the way of behaving of undermined or imperiled species illuminate natural surroundings the executives and preservation endeavors. Understanding searching propensities, movement examples, and reproducing ways of behaving helps plan compelling preservation plans.

   Populace Checking: Social information gathered through current advancements and field perceptions empower the observing of natural life populaces. Traditionalists can follow populace size, regenerative achievement, and the effect of ecological changes on conduct.

   Preservation Brain science: Incorporating mental standards with ethology, protection brain research investigates human-creature cooperations, perspectives, and inspirations. This information can impact public help for preservation drives and advance dependable way of behaving toward natural life.

   Human-Natural life Struggle Relief: Ethological experiences into creature conduct illuminate methodologies for moderating contentions among people and untamed life. Understanding the way of behaving of species that come into contact with human settlements is critical for limiting negative communications.

2. **Grasping Human Way of behaving**

The continuous mission for understanding creature ways likewise has suggestions for how we might interpret human way of behaving.

Developmental Brain science: The investigation of creature conduct adds to the field of transformative brain research, which looks at human conduct with regards to our transformative history. This approach investigates what tribal ways of behaving and variations have meant for human brain science, insight, and social elements.

Social Development: Experiences from social ethology and the investigation of creature customs have affected the field of social advancement in people. Scientists inspect the transmission of ways of behaving, customs, and social practices inside and between human populaces.

Preservation of Human Way of behaving: The investigation of creature conduct can move rehearses that advance maintainable and dependable human way of behaving, especially with regards to asset use, participation, and social association. This approach accentuates the significance of grasping human ways of behaving that influence the climate.

10.4 Future Directions in the Field

Ethology, the logical investigation of creature conduct, has gone through huge development since its origin. From the early spearheading work of Konrad Lorenz and Nikolaas Tinbergen to contemporary progressions in the investigation of creature conduct, ethology has persistently adjusted to embrace new advancements, inter-disciplinary joint effort, and novel exploration questions. As we plan ahead, a few energizing and promising headings in the area of ethology are arising. These future headings include imaginative exploration draws near, the utilization of state of the art innovations, and a more profound comprehension of the mind boggling transaction between conduct, hereditary qualities, and the climate. In this exposition, we will investigate a portion of the key future headings that will shape the area of ethology before long.

Genomics and Conduct Hereditary qualities

Quite possibly of the most encouraging future bearing in ethology is the co-ordination of genomics and conduct hereditary qualities. With progressions in DNA sequencing advances, analysts are presently ready to investigate the hereditary premise of conduct at remarkable degrees of detail. Understanding how qualities impact conduct opens up new roads for research and gives bits of knowledge into the development of ways of behaving.

1. **Far reaching Affiliation Studies (GWAS):** GWAS have been urgent in recognizing explicit qualities related with complex ways of behaving. By breaking down the genomes of people with various social characteristics, specialists can pinpoint hereditary variations that might impact conduct.
2. **Epigenetics and Conduct:** The investigation of epigenetic changes, for example, DNA methylation, offers bits of knowledge into how ecological variables

can impact quality articulation and, subsequently, conduct. Epigenetics adds one more layer of intricacy to the hereditary underpinnings of conduct.

3. **Relative Genomics:** Near genomics permits specialists to look at the hereditary profiles of various species with shifting ways of behaving. This approach distinguishes preserved hereditary components related with explicit social characteristics and adds to how we might interpret conduct advancement.

Neuroethology and Neurogenomics

The eventual fate of ethology likewise includes further investigation of the brain instruments that underlie creature conduct. Neuroethology, the investigation of the brain premise of conduct, is ready to take huge steps in understanding how the cerebrum controls and balances ways of behaving.

1. **High level Mind Imaging:** The improvement of cutting edge cerebrum imaging strategies, for example, useful attractive reverberation imaging (fMRI) for creatures, will empower specialists to plan brain action related with explicit ways of behaving in remarkable detail.

2. **Optogenetics:** Optogenetics is a notable innovation that permits scientists to control brain movement with accuracy utilizing light. Ethologists can utilize optogenetics to explore the causal connection between unambiguous brain circuits and conduct.

3. **Social Genomics:** Incorporating genomics and neurobiology, conduct genomics tries to figure out the hereditary underpinnings of brain advancement and capability. This approach will give a thorough perspective on how qualities impact the construction and capability of the cerebrum, shaping way of behaving.

Mental Ethology and Near Insight

The investigation of creature comprehension, known as mental ethology, is one more thrilling future course in the field. Ethologists are progressively perceiving the mental refinement of creatures, and exploration in this space vows to reveal exceptional experiences into the mental cycles of different species.

1. **Critical thinking and Advancement:** The investigation of critical thinking and development in creatures uncovers their capacity to adjust to novel difficulties. Ethologists are conceiving imaginative trials to examine creatures' ability for development and critical thinking.

2. **Memory and Learning:** The investigation of creature memory and learning keeps on growing comprehension we might interpret how creatures get, hold, and apply information. Memory research in ethology can offer bits of knowledge into how previous encounters shape future way of behaving.

3. **Mathematical Cognizance:** The investigation of mathematical comprehension in creatures has picked up speed. Analysts are analyzing creatures' capacities to figure out amounts, perform essential math undertakings, and make mathematical qualifications. This field features the mental intricacy of creatures.

Ethoecology and the Effect of Environmental Change

As the impacts of environmental change become more articulated, the investigation of creature conduct inside the setting of changing conditions is a critical future heading in ethology. Ethoecology, which investigates the transaction among conduct and biology, will assume a pivotal part in understanding how creatures adjust to and adapt to natural movements.

1. **Environment Actuated Conduct Changes:** Ethologists will progressively explore what environmental change means for creature conduct. This remembers shifts for transient examples, changes in regenerative ways of behaving, and variations to adjusted food accessibility.
2. **Protection Conduct:** Understanding the social reactions of imperiled species to ecological changes is indispensable for their preservation. Ethoecological examination can illuminate versatile administration methodologies to safeguard weak populaces.
3. **Versatility and Variation:** Analysts will investigate how creatures show flexibility and flexibility despite natural difficulties. Experiences from ethoecology can be utilized to anticipate the potential for species to make due in evolving environments.

Interdisciplinary Coordinated effort and Social Ethology

Future bearings in ethology will include upgraded interdisciplinary joint effort. Ethologists will progressively work close by scientists from different fields, like human sciences, social science, and brain research, to acquire a more exhaustive comprehension of creature conduct, remembering the job of culture for shaping way of behaving.

1. **Social Ethology:** Social ethology analyzes the social variety in creature conduct inside and between populaces. Analysts research how learned ways of behaving, customs, and social practices can impact the advancement of conduct.
2. **Ethnozoology:** Ethnozoology, which includes the investigation of human-creature connections in various social orders, gives bits of knowledge into how social convictions and practices shape cooperations with creatures. Coordinated efforts among ethologists and ethnozoologists can uncover the impact of culture on both human and creature conduct.

Ethology and Man-made reasoning

The convergence of ethology with man-made consciousness (computer based intelligence) is a future course that holds extraordinary commitment. Simulated intelligence can be utilized to break down and model complex creature ways of behaving, making it a significant device for ethologists.

1. **Social Investigation:** computer based intelligence and AI calculations can break down tremendous datasets of creature conduct, distinguishing examples, patterns, and social qualities that may not be obvious to the natural eye. This computerized examination speeds up research in ethology.

2. **Independent Information Assortment:** artificial intelligence controlled drones, mechanical stages, and sensor organizations can be utilized to gather information on creature conduct in remote or testing conditions. These innovations give a way to notice and screen creatures without direct human presence.

3. **Displaying Creature Conduct:** artificial intelligence driven demonstrating can recreate creature ways of behaving, giving important experiences into how ways of behaving may develop under various circumstances. These models can be utilized to anticipate the effect of natural changes on creature conduct.